MW00997581

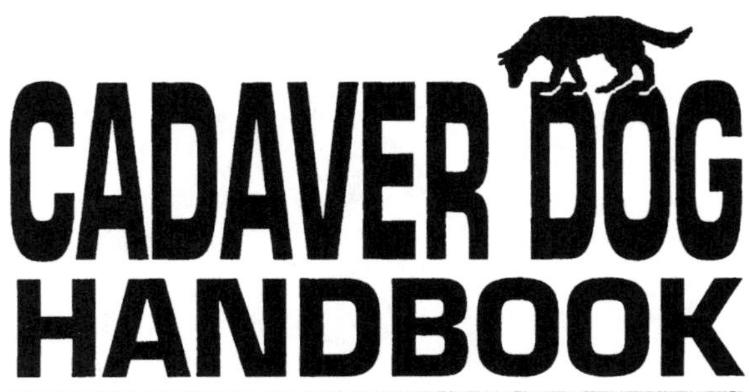

Forensic Training and Tactics for the Recovery of Human Remains

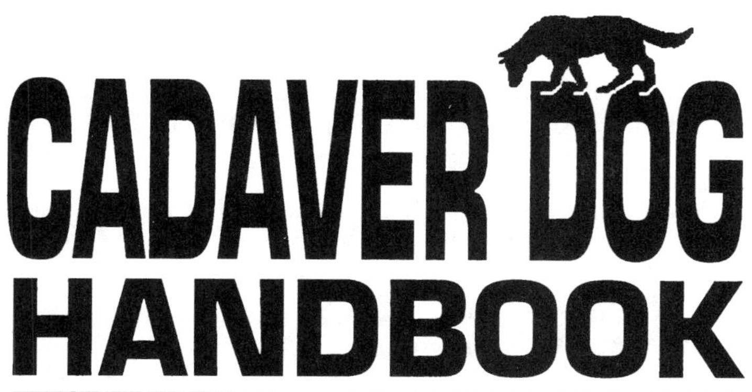

CADAVER DOG HANDBOOK

Forensic Training and Tactics for the Recovery of Human Remains

Andrew Rebmann
Edward David
Marcella H. Sorg

CRC Press
Boca Raton London New York Washington, D.C.

Library of Congress Cataloging-in-Publication Data

Rebmann, Andrew J.
Cadaver dog handbook : forensic training and tactics for the recovery of human remains /Andrew J. Rebmann, Edward David, Marcella H. Sorg, with Marcia Koenig; illustrations and book design, Judith Cooper.
p. cm.
Includes bibliographical references and index.
ISBN 0-8493-1886-6 (alk. paper)
1. Police dogs--Training. 2. Forensic anthropology. I. David, Edward. II. Sorg, Marcella H. III. Koenig, Marcia. IV. Title.

HV8025 .R43 2000
636.7'0886—dc21 00-042900
CIP

Direct all inquiries to CRC Press LLC, 2000 N.W. Corporate Blvd., Boca Raton, Florida 33431.

Visit the CRC Press Web site at www.crcpress.com

International Standard Book Number 0-8493-1886-6
Library of Congress Card Number 00-042900
Printed in the United States of America 5 6 7 8 9 0
Printed on acid-free paper

ACKNOWLEDGMENTS

We would like to thank the Connecticut State Police for their forward thinking and openness to the early cadaver search efforts and training. Since then, dog teams in State Police units, local police, the FBI, and search and rescue groups have contributed to this developing field. There have been many students and colleagues who have made our work possible. We thank them all. We would particularly like to mention Marcia Koenig who not only authored one of the chapters of this book, but, more importantly, is the business partner and spouse to one of us (AR).

The training materials that have been incorporated into these pages evolved over the years with much input. Ideas for some of the illustrations came from the work of Bob Koenig.

We are grateful to the Maine State Police Criminal Investigation Division, State Warden's Service, and Office of Chief Medical Examiner, especially Chief Henry F. Ryan, who consistently supported the use of cadaver dogs in forensic casework. We would also like to acknowledge other Maine handlers and trainers who added their knowledge and ideas in conversations and practice over the years, including Warden Specialist Deborah Palman. We thank Retired State Police K-9 Trainer Lloyd Williams who has been a key supporter and an ongoing source of wisdom.

Finally, and especially, we thank our dogs past and present: Rufus, Lady, Josie, Marianne, Griz, Orca, Coyote, Shadow, Wraith, and Shadow Too (in advance).

DEDICATION

To Clem (who didn't like dead people) and Rufus (who did).
And for Shadow and Marianne (who never got enough).
And for Orca and Coyote.

TABLE OF CONTENTS

ABOUT THE AUTHORS AND CONTRIBUTORS

The authors of this text bring a combined total of over 60 years of experience in forensic casework, national recognition, and a broad, interdisciplinary approach to this topic.

Andrew Rebmann, A.S., retired trooper and K-9 trainer with the Connecticut State Police, has participated in over 1000 cadaver dog searches. He is a cadaver dog trainer with K-9 Specialty Search Associates, of Kent, Washington, and is internationally recognized as a leader in this field. Involved in search work and K-9 training since 1972, he has trained dogs for patrol, narcotics, explosives, arson, wilderness, water, and cadaver work, and has instructed at numerous conferences, seminars and training schools.

Edward David, M.D., J.D., a Deputy Chief Medical Examiner of Maine and experienced cadaver dog handler, has lectured and published on cadaver dog use and outdoor scene processing. He brings to the topic a unique background combining law, medicine, and 20 years of experience in medico-legal death investigation.

Marcella H. Sorg, Ph.D., DABFA, a forensic anthropologist since 1977, and a past-president of the American Board of Forensic Anthropology, has focused multidisciplinary research attention on outdoor scenes, including the interpretation of the postmortem interval, the recovery of human remains, and the role of cadaver dogs.

Marcia Koenig, a former high school and adult education instructor, has been involved in volunteer search dog work since 1972. She was a founding member of the American Rescue Dog Association and the Texas Unit of ARDA, is a founding member of Northwest Disaster Search Dogs and King County Search Dogs, and is a member of both the Puget

Sound FEMA Task Force and the Region 10 DMORT Task Force. She has taught at NASAR and numerous training schools, seminars, and workshops, as well as authored many articles and produced videotapes on dog training.

PREFACE

This handbook on training and working the cadaver dog will fill the void in knowledge available to canine handlers. Who better to author it than Andy Rebmann, Dr. Edward David, and Dr. Marcella Sorg?

I first met Andy in 1980. He was handling a cadaver dog for the Connecticut State Police and instructing at the Maine Police Academy. Andy had his own ideas on training, which proved over the years to become the norm for all canine handlers. His easy-going nature fit nicely with the positive methods of canine training. During my career with the Maine State Police, administering and training for the canine unit from 1979 to 1986, one of the schools I attended was a canine narcotic detection school that Andy instructed. He continually observed and evaluated dogs' and handlers' behavior to better their communication skills and the structure of learning.

I met Dr. David after my retirement from the State Police, as I was starting my own private training facility at Bear Brook Kennels in Brewer, Maine. Dr. David's vast knowledge in the medical field, military background, and position as the Maine Deputy Chief Medical Examiner brought him to me seeking a cadaver dog. I did the original motivation training on "Wraith," his first cadaver dog. We then began the process of teaching him to handle the dog. Well, if you're about to read this handbook, you probably already know that training is 90% handler training and 10% dog training. Dr. David's determination to learn handling techniques has been limited only by his physical handicaps (a back problem limits quick movement, which slows the response time for rewards for the finds). As I look back over the last eight years and the positive results of our work together, I find the second author's credentials verified.

In order to get the whole message from a book like this you need Dr. Marcella Sorg's views and reflections. She makes the effort to investigate and deduce the reasons for what might have happened from the anthropologist's point of view. Dr. Sorg has 22 years working as the state's forensic anthropologist. For the last decade she has been working regularly on cases involving cadaver dogs. She has gathered the data from outdoor searches and the relationship between search techniques and types of postmortem processes.

From my standpoint as a canine trainer, this book will inform the novice of the complexity of the process. To the working handler of cadaver dogs, you will better understand areas of training and working the dog that you never quite fully understood before. To my fellow trainers, it provides the official outline on how we get from green dog and handler to finding cadavers in the field.

Lloyd D. Williams
Master Trainer

CHAPTER 1

INTRODUCTION

SETTING THE STAGE

One of the biggest challenges a forensic investigator may face is the location of the remains of a missing person. The incident may evolve from an apparent suicide, an untimely or accidental death, or a victim of a violent crime. The information available may place the scene in the water, above ground in wooded terrain, or an urban setting, or buried in a known or suspected location.

During the past decade, advances in technology have provided many sophisticated tools to assist the investigator with the location and identification of human remains. Aircraft-mounted infrared detectors, ground penetrating radar, and electromagnetic sensors are just a few that can be used to identify potential gravesites or aboveground victims. Graphing sonar, side-scan sonar, and underwater video equipment have proven beneficial during water searches.

Each of these tools has limitations. Some are cumbersome and suitable for use in small areas. Graphing interpretation requires a high level of expertise, which may not be available. However, when they are combined with another readily available resource, a cadaver dog, they can be used very effectively.

DEFINITION OF CADAVER DOGS

Cadaver dogs are canines, *Canis familiaris,* which are specially trained to find human decomposition scent and alert their handlers to its location. They are used in a variety of forensic contexts, including search and discovery of human cadavers, body parts, or body fluids. In contrast to bloodhounds or other tracking dogs which locate a specific scent on the ground or on an item, cadaver dogs are trained to detect generic scent in the air. In particular, these dogs are conditioned to give an *alert* to the scent of human (as opposed to other animal) decomposition. They are sensitive to the odor given off by bodies dead only a short time, bodies which may lack any obvious signs of decomposition. They will also alert to decomposing bodies, to skeletal remains, or even to soil contaminated with human decomposition fluids. Because of the sensitivity of air scent dog olfaction, even buried bodies or bodies dead for 20 or more years can be detected in certain circumstances. Similarly, objects once in contact with dead bodies can sometimes be identified.

A BRIEF HISTORY OF CADAVER DOGS

The first dog trained exclusively for cadaver search by a police department began work in 1974. The New York State Police were investigating a homicide in Oneida County that involved multiple buried victims in a large forested area. Tpr. R. D. "Jim" Suffolk and "Pearl," a yellow labrador, were trained at the Southwest Research Institute, a military research facility in San Antonio, Texas. Her first find was part of a multiple homicide, the body of a Syracuse College student that was buried four feet deep.

The Connecticut State Police instituted a training program for cadaver search dogs in 1977. Initial emphasis was placed on searching for victims above ground. Since the canine unit was involved in a wide variety of investigations, the focus soon expanded to include buried bodies.

In 1978, TFC Andrew Rebmann of the Connecticut State Police Canine Unit, in conjunction with the State Police laboratory and the Connecticut State Department of Health, Pathology Division, began experimenting with the use of chemical scent sources for the initial training. This training technique is now used for all cadaver dogs attending their program.

Today, specialty dogs are maintained by a number of police departments. There are also over 100 volunteer search dog units who perform cadaver searches.

PURPOSE OF THIS BOOK

Although the training and handling of cadaver dogs shares some characteristics with other evidence dog training and handling, many aspects are unique. Specifically, there are differences between (1) air scent versus tracking dog and (2) human decomposition scent detection versus other scents. Additionally, there are differences in the particular types of search contexts, the patterned nature of the human remains depositions, the specific types of training aids and exercises needed, and the types of handler skills that must be developed.

There has been a recent increase in interest and demand for training and handling information, as well as for standardization and professionalization of training and handling methods. The misapplication and incorrect handling of cadaver dogs has occasionally resulted in failed searches and distrust on the part of some investigators. Such errors are unfortunate. They needlessly dilute the overall capacity of effectiveness of forensic death investigation.

Increasingly, the cadaver dog/handler unit is part of a multidisciplinary search team including medical examiner, anthropologist, and law enforcement members, among others. The coordination of search and evidence/body recovery efforts requires complex strategies, cooperation, and an understanding of the strengths and weaknesses of each team member's potential contribution. It is for these reasons we have produced this handbook, specifically to (1) provide a standard training and handling manual; (2) correct misunderstandings about both the limits and capabilities of cadaver dog searches; and (3) provide a reference for other disciplines involved in evidence/body search and recovery.

OVERVIEW OF BOOK TOPICS AND ORGANIZATION

This handbook is organized to meet a range of needs. Chapters 2, 3, and 4 focus on the basics of understanding scent, canine olfaction, and the ABC's of training and training equipment. Chapters 5 and 6 are focused on the forensic context, including the demands of professionalism and the legal issues surrounding cadaver dog searches. Chapters 7 and 8 present the factors involved in handling a search request and an overview of search context types. Chapter 9 introduces the basics of postmortem processes, including decomposition, disarticulation, and the effects of a variety of taphonomic agents on human remains. Chapters 10, 11, and 12 present guidelines for conducting searches on land and water.

Appendix A provides a list of resources and contacts for training, training aids, and professional education. Appendix B has samples of search reports. Appendix C provides examples of a handler resume and a canine resume.

CHAPTER 2

DOG BASICS

THE WORKING DOG

The domestic dog, *Canis familiaris,* is one of 38 species in the family Canidae. Other members of this family include the wolf, coyote, fox, jackal, and others. All canids have large canine teeth, blunt, non-retractable claws with five toes on the fore feet and four toes on the hind feet, and a long muzzle. Canids are found throughout the world with the exception of Antarctica.

Members of the dog family evolved from a weasel-like, tree-climbing carnivorous ancestor, *Miacis*, during the Eocene Epoch. Dogs are most closely linked in the evolutionary sense with cats and are sometimes placed in the same superfamily. Approximately 38 million years ago, during the Oligocene Epoch, approximately 50 forerunners of today's canids appeared. Eight million years ago during the Pliocene Epoch the first wolves and foxes appeared. Other canids, represented today by the hyena, branched off from *Miacis* early on, closer to the Eocene.

There are eight species in the genus *Canis*. *C. lupis* is the chief member, having once ranged throughout Europe, Asia, and North America. *C. niger,* the red wolf, lives in the southeastern United States and is on the endangered species list. The coyote, *C. latrans*, is a rapidly expanding member of the genus and is found throughout the United States and Canada, excepting Hawaii. There are four species of jackal, none in North America. The domestic dog has evolved from the gray wolf, *C. lupis*.

The American Kennel Club (AKC) currently recognizes 147 breeds of dog. There are seven groups recognized by the AKC. The "working" dog term as used in this book is not synonymous with the Working group of the AKC. Many of the dogs used in air scent work come from the Herding group, however, which was a part of the AKC Working group until 1983. Working air scent dogs come from many of the AKC groups as well as being of mixed ancestry.

What defines the working dog is its combination of body build, stamina, and drive. The choice of body build is in part a reflection of the environment in which the dog will work. A heavy-coated dog, for example, is not the appropriate choice for the southwestern United States desert region. Similarly, a short-coated dog will do poorly in the cold northern parts of the country. Temperature and terrain also affect the choice regarding size. Caloric expenditure and heat dissipation are functions of size. All other things being equal, a smaller dog will do better in a warmer environment.

A working dog must have significant stamina. Search terrain, weather, other environmental factors, and the length of a search all combine to require a certain amount of stamina. Stamina is as much a result of the care given a dog as it is its genes. A dog that is not exercised, or is overweight and undertrained will do poorly. It must be stated, however, that too much exercise too early may result in bone problems in many breeds. An overweight dog also may fall prey to degenerative bone problems, severely impacting its search stamina.

The sex of the dog should also be considered, although temperament is ultimately more important. In other words, there are behavioral differences between the sexes as a whole, but there is more overlap than difference. If the dog is going to be used for air scent work there may be reasons to choose a female. Generally, although not always, females are easier to control. If you are not a full-time or experienced trainer or handler, this might make preparing and handling the dog less difficult. Females tend to want to please more than males and are only rarely dominant over male dogs. This, when coupled with their smaller size, may be a major advantage. And, it may be important if the dog is going to be introduced into a household with other dogs. Finally, females tend to have a softer temperament and may not require as firm a correction; however, when corrected, they may shut down more readily than a male. In sum, sex is one of many considerations, but it is important to remember that individual dogs may not fall into these broad patterns.

Hormonal issues should also be considered. A female is going to come into season twice a year. During that time the dog cannot be used to search. This is not because the dog is unable to perform, but because being in heat will attract all male dogs in the vicinity and will interfere with the working of other dogs involved in the search. If you do not intend to breed your dog, you should have it spayed. The problem with a male dog is its response to any female in heat. When detected, this will be a major, work-threatening distraction to a male dog.

The most important consideration is drive. If the dog is being chosen solely for air scent work, the principal drive is the *prey drive.* Basically, you should look for a dog that is "ball crazy." The dog should follow the movement of the ball and the dog should have a good grip on the ball when it catches it.

Several tests can be made, particularly with puppies, to get a sense of the dog's mental state. The dog should be removed to a new environment and observed. Is the dog upset by the change, or is the dog adaptive? A dog that is not adaptive within a few minutes could be a problem. If the dog is adaptive, then something should be done to startle it; a loud noise is best. The startle should not involve rapid movement on your part. The dog should recover quickly and either investigate the source of the noise or go about its business. A dog that either cowers or runs will be a problem down the road. Removed from its surroundings, does a dog follow you or run away and ignore you? While ignoring you may be a sign of independence, which is worthwhile in a search animal, it could also be a clue of difficulties ahead in terms of obedience. A dog that appears nervous and constantly tries to return to its run probably should not be considered.

The authors feel that the selection of a working dog is one of the most important choices a person will make. Unless you are a breeder or a professional trainer it makes sense to do the following:

- Deal only with breeder's having a solid reputation.
- Enlist the services of a qualified professional trainer in your selection process, someone who makes their living evaluating and training dogs.
- Have your potential new working partner checked by a veterinarian, preferably one with long experience dealing with working dogs.

DOG NOSES AND DOG BRAINS

It is helpful to have some understanding of the anatomy and physiology involved in a dog's scent work. This can help to explain why a dog is working well or not working at all. It will also give the handler a better insight into the effects of the environment on a search.

Problems within the sense of smell can be difficult to test. A handler's observation of a dog's behavior can be quite reliable however. If a dog does not seem to be working well, some tests can be performed. Sample hides of known strength can be used to test the dog. Irritant substances should not be used. As will be explained below, these substances do not test the sense of smell, but rather act on nerve endings designed to sense pain.

While one can develop an extensive list of the causes of loss of smell (anosmia), far and away the most common cause will be a rhinitis. This may be due to infection, irritation, or allergy. Irritation will usually be a factor only when an environmental irritant is present in the search area, i.e., at a dump site or a scene where volatile chemicals have played a role, such as at an air crash. The second most probable cause is head injury. The olfactory nerves are subject to shear where they pass through the cribriform plate (see Figures 2.1 and 2.2).

All animals directly sense chemical molecules. This is true even in animals that lack a nose. Bacteria are known to sense and cluster about certain chemicals. Flies sense molecules through their feet. Sea run fish such as Atlantic salmon probably return to their original spawning areas using smell. Mammals vary widely in their ability to smell. This correlates with the number of receptor cells in the nose and olfactory bulb. Human beings have approximately 5 million olfactory receptor cells. A bloodhound has 100 million such cells. Interestingly, this correlation between ability to smell and the number of receptor cells does not hold when comparing mammals with other animals. Thus, certain bird species with a remarkable sense of smell have been found to have a limited number of receptor cells.

Age related changes do occur. Atrophic features can be found in older dogs. They are found in the company of other changes associated with "senile brain changes." The changes have been found in dogs ranging in age from 10 to 19 years. Significant change, however, was not found in any dog less than 14 years old. Age should not be a consideration, as most dogs will have been retired from active searching before scent discrimination becomes an issue.

The nasal structure in dogs mediates three distinct functions. These are respiration, olfaction, and accessory olfaction. Respiration is

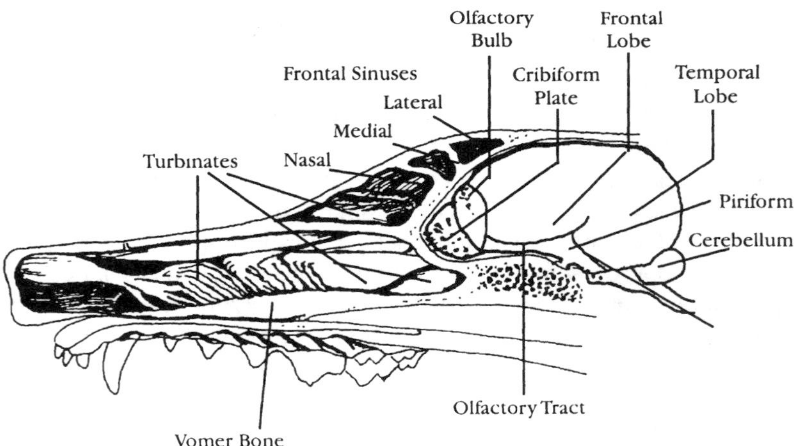

Figure 2.1 Partial dog skull, illustrating nasal cavity and anterior brain (midline section, view from side, nasal septum removed in order to show turbinates)

accomplished by the drawing in and expelling out of air through the nose. The air is moistened passing over the nasal structures.

The olfactory system consists of the soft tissue, bone, nerves, and portions of the brain. The soft tissue and bony structures create cavities into which air and the odors it carries are drawn. The cavities are lined with receptor cells which in turn connect to olfactory nerves.

The accessory olfactory system deals with recognition of other dogs, territory, and sex. It is mediated through the vomeronasal organs. These are cigar-shaped small bodies located on the floor of the nasal cavity. Dogs use their tongues to transfer material from a source to the vomeronasal organ. Urine and feces contain odor cues that aid in identification and/or detecting the presence of another animal. The marks also define home-range territories.

Dogs can detect how recently a scent has been placed in a given location. They may use visual displays in association with marking. Thus a male dog may use raised-leg urination to mark an area rather than giving an alert. This gives both an olfactory and a visual warning to any other dogs searching the area. Similarly, the dog may scratch the ground following urination or defecation. This probably is done to leave an additional olfactory mark utilizing the interdigital scent glands. Again, the message is for other dogs to stay out of this area. The handler must be aware of this behavior or odor sources may be missed.

The main olfactory system of the dog is highly sensitive. It allows for the detection of a wide range of odors under difficult conditions. Dogs are able to discriminate the searched-for odor in an environment full of distracting odors.

The dog's anatomy is a remarkably good design. There is an elongated snout with folding of the turbinate bones to increase surface area. The nostrils open into paired nasal cavities. A medial septum separates these cavities. It is partially supported by cartilage. The lateral (on the sides) walls contain the turbinate bones. Each bone takes its name from the facial bone of which it is a part. The nasoturbinate is a fairly simple structure running the length of the nares. The maxillary turbinate is complex in the dog with numerous folds running from the front upwards and from the back downwards. The ethmoid turbinates contain the specialized olfactory receptor epithelium. This epithelium or layer of tissue consists of several types of cells. The olfactory receptor neurons have cilia bathed in mucus, over which the stimuli flow. Supporting cells and basal cells surround the neurons.

The neural connections of the olfactory system are basically of two types. The first type to be discussed below deals with the primary recognition of odor. The second type (which will not be discussed here) deals with the "emotional" functions associated with odors. This second type has rich connections with the vomeronasal organ. It involves the limbic system and becomes even more prominent in primates (monkeys, apes, and humans).

The primary olfactory pathway begins with the olfactory receptor neurons. The axons join together to form the olfactory nerve or the first cranial nerve. The nerve passes through holes in the cribriform plate. The nerve then passes into the olfactory bulb where it has its first synapse. Many olfactory neurons converge on a fewer number of olfactory bulb neurons. Axons from the olfactory bulb project through the olfactory track to the olfactory cortex in the brain on the same side. Synapses occur between neurons in the olfactory peduncle, lateral striae, or olfactory tubercle. The majority of these projections do not relay in the brain's thalamus, but pass directly to the pyriform cortex. Commissures at various points in the pathway beneath the olfactory bulbs correlate the two separate inputs from the olfactory neurons.

How does this all work? It appears that smell receptors on the olfactory neurons in the nose bond to molecules in the air passing over the neurons. Studies have shown that there are distinctly different routes of airflow when a dog is merely breathing as opposed to when the dog is sniffing. With sniffing, a considerably greater amount of air is drawn over the olfactory mucosa. The molecules cause the receptors to send electrical signals to the olfactory bulb and then to the appropriate parts of the cortex. The criteria responsible for neuronal firing remain under study. Some of the more important factors appear to be the overall size and shape of the molecule. Additionally the stereo chemistry of the molecule and certain chemical and physical properties must be important. Physical properties that probably have significance include solubility and volatility. Chemical properties of importance probably include polarity and the nature of functional groups. The latter would be particularly important in smaller molecules. The genetics and biochemistry of smell are just beginning to be understood.

One interesting point is the number of receptors involved in smell. Color vision requires only three types of receptor. Taste probably requires no more than five receptors. Smell requires 1000 receptors. This seemingly large number is admittedly small, however, when compared to the number of odors in the world around us. Each odor does not require its own receptor. Receptors bond to one or several molecules depending on their shape. The receptors also overlap. Many will respond to the same odorant. Complex scents are made up of many odorant molecules. These different molecules cause a different firing pattern to occur, which is unique to the total odor. This allows the training of a dog for scent-specific work.

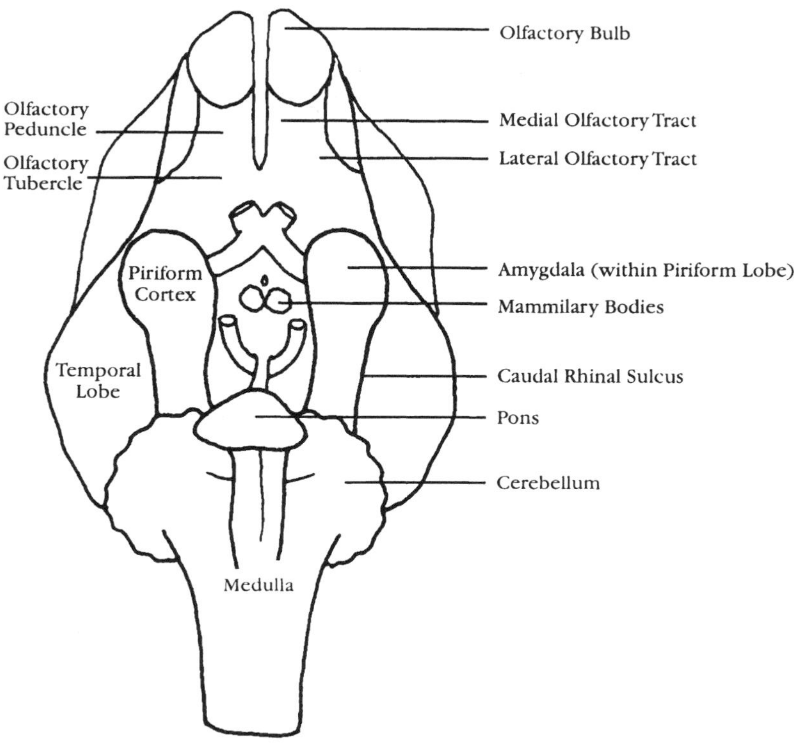

Figure 2.2 Dog brain, illustrating olfactory system (view from bottom)

SCENT CONE THEORY

Training for cadaver search requires the handler to have a working knowledge of scent, including its origin and its transmission to, and behavior in, the environment.

Scent is produced when molecules from an object are dispersed into the air and register a sensory reaction in the brain. Molecules shed by the object become more and more dispersed the farther away from it they move. This concentration gradient theoretically forms a scent cone (see Figure 2.3). The scent within the cone is stronger the closer one moves to the object, owing to the increased concentration of the scent molecules. In contrast, the scent farther away from the object is fainter and more diffuse.

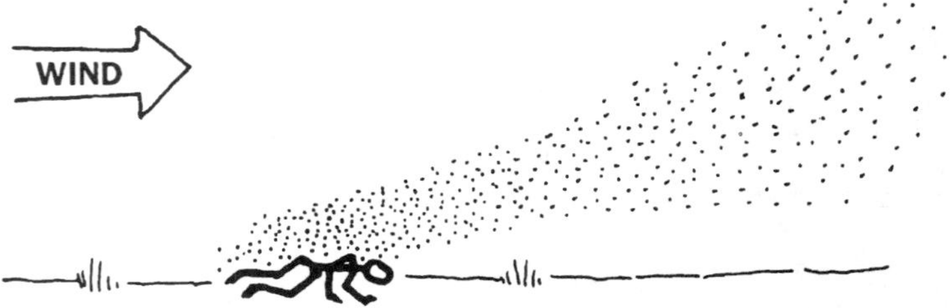

Figure 2.3 Primary scent cone

Mammals are able to detect both the presence and the relative concentration of scent. That is, they are able to discriminate and follow a pattern of increasing concentration to its source at the apex of the scent cone.

Interruptions to and enhancements of the spread of molecules from the source may distort the scent cone. For example, wind currents may move scent molecules far from their source, and objects in the environment may trap the molecules and prevent them from moving. The model of the ideal scent cone and the principles of environmental scent cone distortion constitute scent cone theory.

Handlers of air scent search dogs should be familiar with how a dog uses airborne odor to locate a subject. Tracking/trailing handlers recognize when their dog is following a scent trail and how wind, weather, terrain, and time can affect the dogs ability to locate the subject. Air scent dog handlers need to understand these basics and how they apply to air scent searching.

Understanding the basic concepts is essential to success. Even a well-trained dog will not perform well without a handler that can guide the process. The dog is able to follow an ideal scent cone model of increasing concentration to the source. But only the handler can analyze the environmental context and its potential scent cone distortions, anticipate the dog's response, and guide the dog appropriately.

"LIVE" SCENT VERSUS "DEATH" SCENT

Though the composition of cadaver scent is different than the odor emitted by a live person, the principles of transmission to and movement in the environment are the same. Thus, dog/handler teams trained well for air-scent search and rescue can apply many of the search principles in cadaver dog searches.

At the time of *biological death,* the individual scent emitted by the subject undergoes a transformation. This change is not immediately detectable by a human; however, it obviously affects the composition of the odor detected by the dog and the resulting behavior. A phenomena that has been noted by many tracking/trailing dog handlers is that some dogs will follow a trail, often many days old, but fail to close in on the body if the subject is deceased. They may register the scent change and, whether from fear, difference in odor, or some other reason, may not approach. If the handler had never observed this behavior before, he or she might assume the dog had lost the scent trail. In reality, the dog is showing aversion to cadaver scent. The dog may show aversion by its hackles raising, circling, or other behavior that indicates that it does not want to approach an area. Through training these behaviors can be overcome.

Cadaver scent differs from live scent. It is chemically generic and not specific to one individual. The chemical reactions associated with decomposition are essentially the same in all bodies. However, cadaver scent is not a single scent, but a range of scents produced during different stages of the decomposition process. The cadaver dog must be trained to recognize and react to this entire spectrum of scent.

The scent picture changes as the body progresses through the decomposition stages and the chemistry changes. It is important to note that dog reactions when introduced to a cadaver scents are very individual to the dog. It is not unusual for a dog to attempt to roll in putrefied matter or mark the substance by urinating or defecating on or near it. Other particular reactions may occur.

In order to understand the type of scent available to the dog, it is important to learn about the stages of decomposition. The *decomposition process* commences immediately after biological death occurs and proceeds through five stages before the body is completely skeletonized.

Certain elements are necessary for the process to occur. These elements affect how rapidly the remains proceed through the various stages.

The decay process produces a variety of gases, liquids, and acids. It is these by-products that provide the odor that the dog is trained to recognize and indicate. There are also two special situations with different scent results: if a body decomposes in a wet environment, there will be the production of *adipocere*. This grayish, soapy substance provides a good scent picture to the dog. If the body is left in a hot, dry environment it will *mummify,* and the odor will be musty. This odor is also recognizable by the animal.

Table 2.1. Stages of decomposition and odor characteristics

Stage	Description	Odor [1]
Fresh	Little or no exterior change; however, is decomposing internally due to bacteria present in the body before death.	None detectable by humans; however, animal may show reaction or approach body as if it were still alive. Dog may detect at some distance.
Bloated	Body swollen by gas produced internally. Insect activity may be apparent.	Decay odor present. Detectable by both dog and human. Can be detected at a distance.
Decay	Body collapses as gas escapes. Exposed flesh may be black.	Strong putrefaction odor detectable by dog and human at some distance.
Liquefaction	Liquids created during the decay process seep into the environment. Body drying out.	Reduced odor production. May smell cheesy or musty. Animal still may detect at a distance.
Dry or Skeletal	Slow rate of decay. Remaining flesh may be mummified.	Musty odor. Detection distance shortened.

[1] Detection distance varies with wind direction, weather, and terrain. If approaching upwind, detection distance will be much greater than if working with the wind at the handler's back.

Table 2.2. Elements of decomposition

Element	Description
Microorganisms	Normally present in the lungs and intestinal tract. Many are necessary in a living person for normal functions. If death is the result of disease, pathological organisms may be present.
Warmth	Decomposition is significant at approximately 50°F and proceeds most rapidly between 70° and 100°F. Between 100° and 212°F, the process slows as the reproduction of bacteria is retarded by the increased temperature and moisture is evaporated.
Air	Oxygen-consuming organism activity is retarded by the absence of air. Restriction of airflow around remains will slow the decomposition process.
Moisture	Microorganisms require moisture to function. A body normally contains enough moisture for the bacteria to multiply.

Thus, as decomposition proceeds, the scent production begins at a low level, proceeds through a very odiferous period, and then subsides again. Dogs should be taught to react to the scent picture through the complete spectrum. And handlers need to understand the relationship between the decomposition process and the potential for its detection in the environment.

SCENT AND THE ENVIRONMENT

Environmental alterations or distortions to scent cones are infinite in variety according to the terrain, vegetation, climate, season, and weather. However, there are a number of principles of scent cone distortion that need to be understood by the handler (see Table 2.3)

Table 2.3. Principles of Scent Cone Presence and Distortion

1. Decomposition odor will tend to form a scent pool above and around the remains.
2. Air flow will move the scent away from the source in the direction of the wind, forming an air scent cone.
3. Water will move the scent away from the source along scent conduits in response to gravity and/or currents, along surface or underground waterways, or following established erosion or drainage patterns.
4. Wind or water flow can be altered by scent barriers, which may cause the formation of secondary scent pools, potentially forming a new, secondary scent cone remote from the remains.
5. Variable wind patterns can cause an uneven distribution of scent molecules in the air and scent cone distortion or breaks.
6. Water flow along a conduit can interrupt the absorption of scent into the soil near the remains (but outside the conduit) causing a scent void near the remains at the dog-nose level.
7. Elevation of the body with a horizontal scent cone can produce a scent void near the remains at the dog-nose level.

DECOMPOSITION ODOR FORMS A SCENT POOL

When air is stagnant and unmoving, the scent tends to pool above and all around decomposing remains, forming a *primary scent pool* (Figure 2.4). Scent molecules are gradually shed into the air and absorbed into the soil in all directions around the body.

WIND CARRIES SCENT AWAY FORMING A SCENT CONE

Homogeneous, directional air movement bears scent molecules away from the source, forming a cone-shaped gradient of decreasing concentration and increasing dispersion (Figure 2.5a). The cone apex is located at the cadaver source where the greatest scent concentration is found. The *horizontal scent cone*'s longitudinal axis extends laterally away from the remains in the direction of the wind. In the absence of detectable wind, air currents due to rising heat can cause scent to ascend into the air above the body forming a vertical scent cone in which scent fails to be dispersed widely around the body (Figure 2.5b).

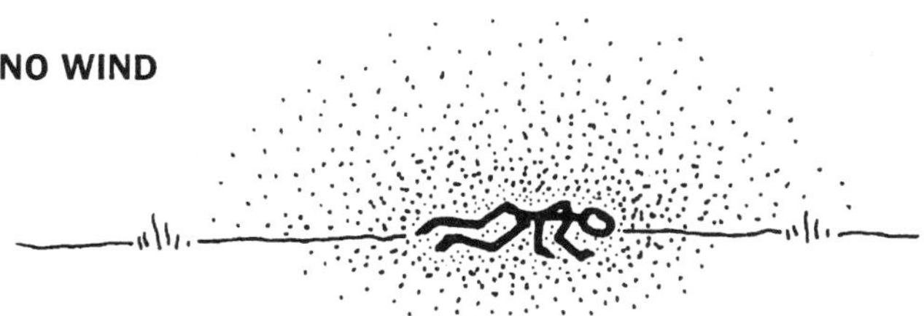

Figure 2.4 Primary scent pool

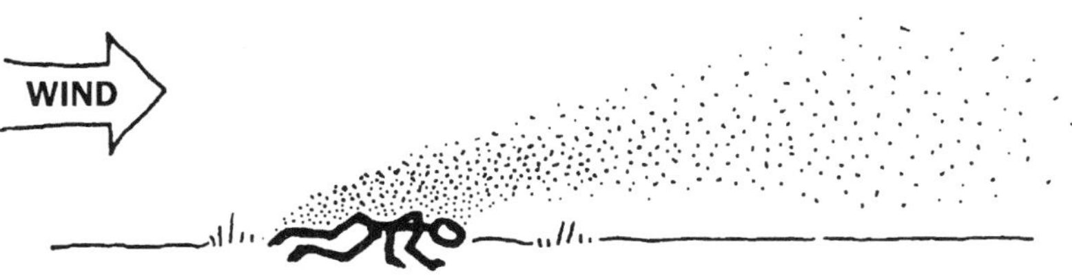

Figure 2.5a Horizontal scent cone due to wind

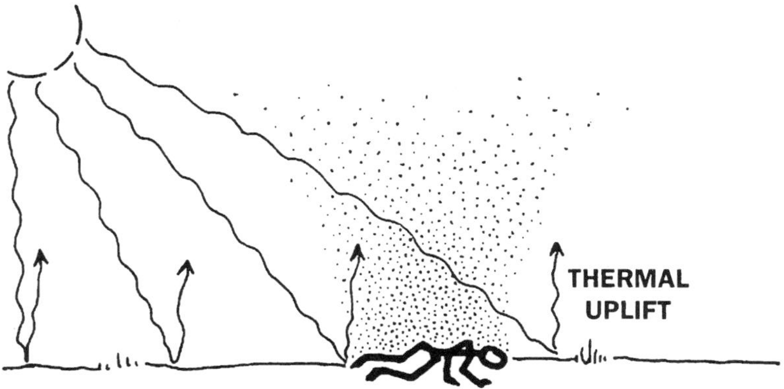

Figure 2.5b Vertical scent cone due to thermal uplift

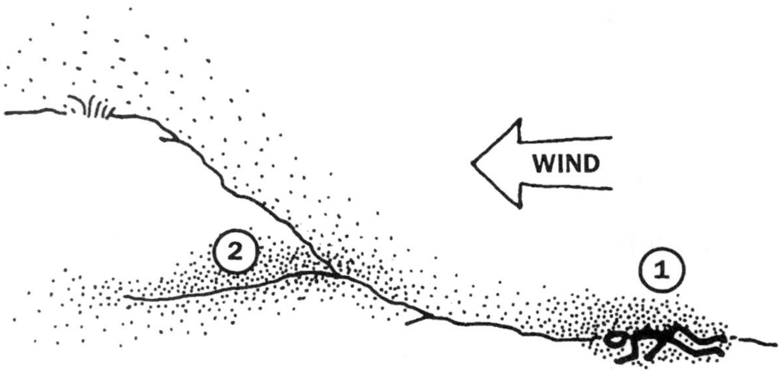

Figure 2.6a Primary and secondary scent pools/cones due to terrain barriers

Figure 2.6b Primary and secondary scent pools/cones due to vegetation barriers

BARRIERS CAUSE SCENT TO FORM SECONDARY SCENT POOLS AND SECONDARY SCENT CONES

Wind-borne scent molecules can change direction or pool at air flow barrier locations, forming *secondary scent cones* remote from the body. For example, scent-bearing wind that hits the side of a hill or a tree can result in a *secondary scent pool* at the base of the hill (Figure 2.6a) or at the base of the tree which can form a new horizontal cone (Figure 2.6b).

WATER MOVES SCENT AWAY FROM THE SOURCE

Scent molecules can be carried by water away from the terrestrially decomposing body by gravity. The scent can be incorporated into draining ground water and be carried along underwater streams, eventually reappearing in areas remote from the body (Figure 2.7). Similarly, scent can drain away from the body along the surface, down a hill, with moving water, reducing absorption into the ground under the body and reducing the concentration of molecules in the scent cone near the body (Figure 2.8).

Water currents carry scent away from a body underwater. Depending on temperature gradients within the water column, the scent can be brought to the surface just above or more remote from the body (Figure 2.9).

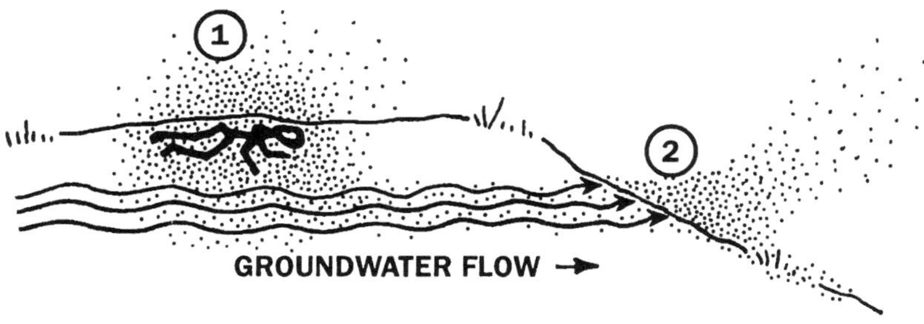

Figure 2.7 Primary and secondary scent pools/cones

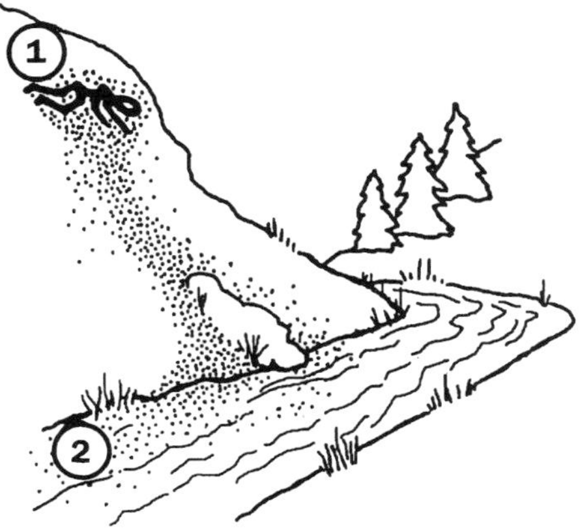

Figure 2.8 Scent washes downhill with surface run-off to stream or secondary scent pool

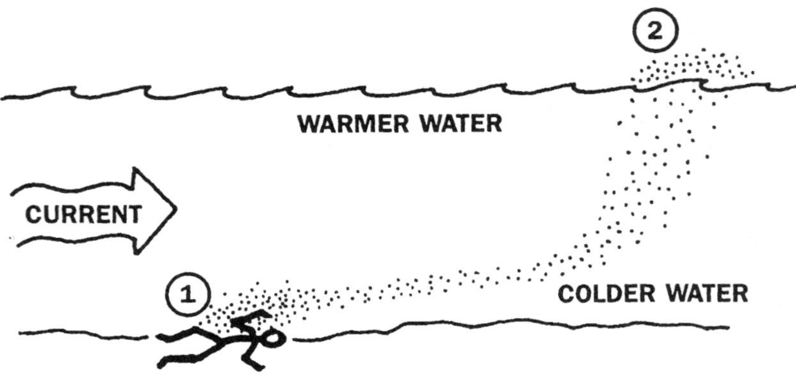

Figure 2.9 Waterborne scent creates a remote scent pool

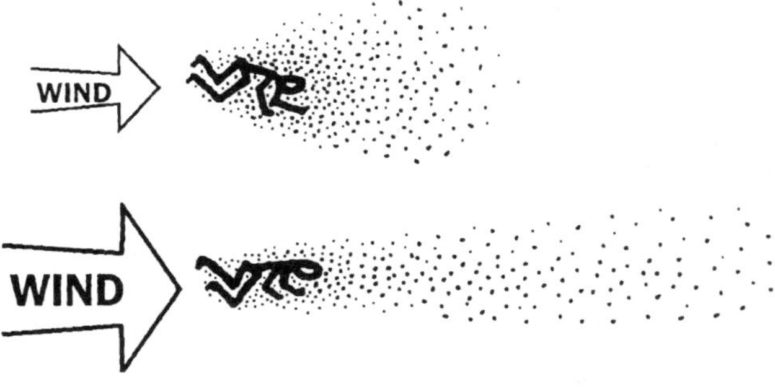

Figure 2.10 Variation in scent cone shape and concentration due to wind speed

SCENT CONE DISTORTION IS PRODUCED BY VARIABLE WINDS

If wind is intermittent and/or multi-directional, the scent cone can be broken up and scent dispersed in non-uniform ways (Figure 2.10). This can bring puffs of scent to the dog that are not continuous back to the body (Figure 2.11). Scent cone distortion can produce faint of partial alerts by the dog.

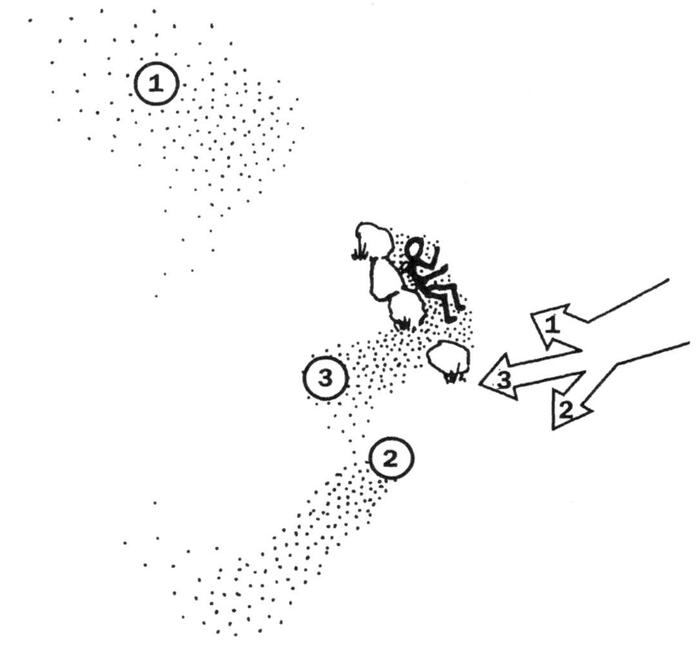

Figure 2.11 Variable scent cone distribution due to light and changing wind

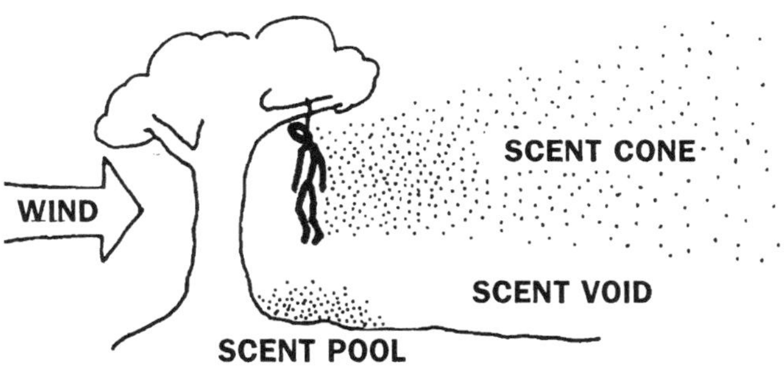

Figure 2.12 Scent void formed with a hanging body

SCENT VOIDS CAN BE PRODUCED IN WATER OR ON LAND

Water currents below the surface can carry away the scent of an underwater body, surfacing at an area remote from the remains, producing a scent void in the water near the body.

Because the dog nose operates within just a couple feet of the ground surface, certain areas can be missed. If a body is elevated, as in a hanging for instance, and the scent cone is horizontal, the apex of the cone cannot be reached by the dog (Figure 2.12). Further, a scent void will be created just to the side of the hanging body, essentially underneath the narrow part of the scent cone. This situation is replicated when the body is on elevated ground.

LIMITS OF CADAVER DOGS AND SCENT DETECTION

The ability of a well-trained cadaver dog to successfully find human remains depends on a number of external factors, including:

- Whether remains are actually present (investigation information)
- Whether remains are creating a scent pool and a scent cone above ground (stage of decomposition, body covering, soil type, and drainage)
- Air movement between the scent pool and the dog (wind direction and speed, dog location relative to body)

- Temperature (above freezing and below approximately 90°F)
- Whether the handler guides the dog to the correct area (handler skill)
- Whether the handler correctly interprets the dog's behavior

In other words, the dog's efforts are only as good as the quality of the pre-search investigation, and the handler's skills; and they are dependent as well on the weather and the environmental characteristics of the search area.

It is important to emphasize that the handler be cognizant of all of these limitations in the interpretation and conclusions regarding a search. *Failure to acknowledge limitations places unrealistic expectations in the minds of others involved in the search and ultimately tarnishes perceptions about the use of cadaver dogs.*

CHAPTER 3

TRAINING THE CADAVER DOG

SELECTION OF A DOG TO TRAIN

The candidate canine must be structurally sound, well socialized, and already under the handler's control. There should be a good bond with the handler. The candidate must also have endurance, the ability to work independently, and a strong reward system response. The dog should have a strong hunt/prey drive. It is a great benefit if the dog has had previous experience with either trailing or air scent search.

HANDLER CHARACTERISTICS NEEDED

- Physical fitness
- Psychological preparation to cope with the results of a search
- Working knowledge of canine training principles
- Good bond with dog
- Ability to cooperate with other members of forensic team
- Ability to keep records and generate reports

OVERVIEW OF TRAINING

Before beginning cadaver specialty search training, the canine/handler team should be experienced in tracking, or air scent area search, or both. A canine/handler team that has had scent training performs better. Also, the handler will be familiar with "reading" the dog's body language.

Training begins by introducing the scent and developing commitment to locate the source. Then the dog is taught to give an easily identifiable indication to the handler that it has located the source; this is termed the *trained alert*. Once the team is working well together, the source is hidden above ground, hung and buried. During training, the team works on problems that become larger and more realistic.

After they have become competent, the team is introduced to water search. The handler is taught to interpret the dog's alert on a source in the water while working either from shore or in a boat.

The handler is instructed in specialty search tactics. The program culminates with proficiency testing for dog and handler. Successful completion of a training program should produce a canine/handler team that can conduct a cadaver search with a high probability of success.

Once the team is trained, competence must be maintained through a regular practice and training program.

TRAINING BASICS

When you begin to teach any new task to your dog, keep in mind the three P's: Patience, Perseverance, and Praise. Animals learn through many repetitions and being rewarded for their performance. Keep the following in mind:

1. Consistently reward at (or as close to) the source as possible. This action strengthens the commitment to the target odor.
2. Mark the desired behavior. Timing of marking is critical. Using a clicker usually allows the trainer better timing and also buys you time to reinforce the dog, since the clicker means a reward is coming. (Clicker training is discussed on page 29.)
3. Make sure the animal is performing consistently at the current level before proceeding to the next.
4. Do not hesitate to work an easier basic exercise if the dog has problems at the current level.
5. Do many repetitions at each level.
6. Vary the location of the scent source in the pattern. If you are using concrete blocks to house the scent, for example, make sure you move the block when you move the scent source.
7. You can add scent sources to the pattern so the dog has the opportunity to indicate more than one source during one repetition of an exercise.

SHAPING BEHAVIOR

When training a dog, most dog handlers are concerned about methods. There are many methods to teach any behavior; some work better than others, and some work better with a particular type of dog than another.

This section, however, focuses on training principles. These principles can be used with any methods; the principles are universal. These principles were discovered primarily by the psychologist B.F. Skinner. He called it *operant conditioning* (or *shaping behavior*). In the 1960s, these principles were used to train dolphins. You cannot put a choke chain around a dolphin's neck. You cannot deprive them of food or they become ill. You cannot force them into doing anything or they will just swim away. So all that trainers were left with was to shape behavior with positive reinforcement.

In the 1980s, Karen Pryor, one of the original dolphin trainers, wrote a book called *Don't Shoot the Dog, the New Art of Teaching and Training*. She put these principles together in a way that would be of practical use to anyone trying to shape any animal from humans to chickens. In the last few years she has been lecturing to dog clubs about shaping dog behavior. The following material is excerpted from Karen Pryor's work.

A Dog and a Dolphin: Training without Punishment

by Karen Pryor

DOGS, DOLPHINS, AND TRAINING

If you've seen trained dolphin shows at oceanariums or on TV, you will know that dolphins appear to be wonderfully trainable. On command they exhibit all kinds of precision behavior, including splendid acrobatics and interactive behavior with other dolphins or with human swimmers. The audience marvels at how eagerly they respond and how intelligent they must be; wouldn't it be nice if dogs responded like that?

As we dolphin trainers know well, the truth is that dolphins aren't geniuses, and neither are dolphin trainers. The dolphins' speed, precision, and obvious enjoyment of their work is due entirely to the principles dolphin trainers use in training them. And the same techniques can be used on dogs.

OMITTING PUNISHMENT FROM THE START

The first thing to understand about dolphin training is that we are working with animals you can't punish. No matter how mad you get—even if the animal makes you mad on purpose, by splashing you from head to foot, say—you can't retaliate.

Maybe you're thinking "I bet I could think up a way to punish a dolphin.." and I bet you could; but it doesn't matter, because dolphin trainers don't need it. Trainers can get whatever they want from a dolphin, using positive reinforcement only: mostly just a chirp or two from a training whistle and a bucket of fish. We "shape" every behavior by *positive reinforcement*. We use positive reinforcement to elicit prompt and correct response to commands—to achieve obedience. We can even use positive reinforcement to discipline an animal—to control misbehavior such as attacking a tank mate or refusing to go through a gate. This sophisticated use of positive reinforcement results in an animal that works brilliantly and loves to work.

The methods we use to train dogs often include the use of force, both to put the dog through required movements and to correct the dog when it makes mistakes, which it inevitably does. Although we may also use praise and petting, unavoidably the dog experiences some confusion, fear, and maybe even physical pain in the training process. Some dogs tolerate these negative experiences well, but dolphins, being wild animals, would not. If you were to train a dolphin by these techniques, the dolphin might learn, but it would offer a sluggish, sulky, unreliable performance; and it might well begin to exhibit aggression toward people. (Does that sound like any dogs you know?)

On the other hand if you train a dog the way we train dolphins, through positive reinforcement, the dog behaves just like a dolphin: it becomes eager, attentive, precise, cooperative, and capable of fantastic performance. Here's how it's done.

THE MAGIC SIGNAL: CONDITIONED REINFORCERS

When I talk to dog trainers a big misconception I run into is that positive reinforcement just means "food." Wrong. The crucial element in getting wonderful behavior out of a dolphin is not the food reward. The dolphin is not working for the fish: the dolphin is working for the whistle. The sound of the whistle is the magic signal that brings about that wonderful performance.

For example, suppose, on several occasions, the dolphin heard the whistle (and later got a fish) when it happened to be jumping in the air. Soon it would start jumping every time the trainer showed up. Then it might be allowed to discover that jumping only "works" when the trainer's arm is raised. So a raised arm becomes the green light, as it were, for jumping.

The trainer could gradually impose other conditions—jumping only "works" when the direction of the jump is away from the trainer and toward the audience; when the jump is higher than four feet; when the jump occurs within three seconds after the arm is raised. At the end of a few training sessions the trainer has trained the dolphin to "take a bow," on command and with precision; and the dolphin has trained the trainer too: "All I have to do is make a certain kind of jump when she sticks her hand up, and she immediately gives me a whistle and a fish every time!"

Note that the whistle is not used as a command. It does not tell the dolphin to start doing something—the hand signal does that. The whistle tells the dolphin, during or at the end of a behavior, that the trainer likes that behavior and the dolphin deserves a fish for it. (You don't have to stick with food, either; you can also associate a conditioned reinforcer with a pat, or a toy, or maybe just another chance to work.)

The whistle has now become a *conditioned reinforcer.* In the language of the psychologist, food, petting, or any other pleasure is an unconditioned reinforcer—something the animal would want, even without training; the whistle, a conditioned reinforcer, is something the animal has learned to want. (Some people use the term "primary reinforcer" for food and "secondary reinforcer" for the signal. I avoid those terms because I find it leads people to think that if the whistle is "secondary" it should occur after the food, which of course makes it meaningless to the animal and useless as a training tool).

WHY THE CONDITIONED REINFORCER IS CRUCIAL

What would happen if you tried to train a dolphin to do a simple jump, away from you, on cue—without the whistle? First, you could not possibly time the fish to arrive when the animal was in mid-jump, so no matter what kind of jump the animal gave, it would either get the fish later or get no fish at all. It would have no way of telling why you rewarded one jump over another or what you liked about the jump. Was it the height? Or maybe the way the animal took off or landed? To develop a jump of a particular height, timing, and direction you would have to eliminate mistakes by trial and error over many, many repetitions; you would be lucky if the animal didn't get bored (and the trainer too!) before the performance was correct and reliable.

Also when a trainer uses food without a conditioned reinforcer the animal is apt to look toward the trainer for food all the time. Horses nose your pockets and dogs lick your hands. Dolphins hang around the training station and worship the fish bucket. And with the animal constantly looking at the trainer it would be difficult to train our dolphin to jump facing away from the trainer, toward the audience. Once you've established the conditioned reinforcer, however, you can use the whistle to reinforce behavior that occurs at a distance, or with the animal facing away from you, with no trouble at all. And the well-conditioned animal, instead of nosing around for a snack, is going on about its business, but also attentively listening for the magic sound, whatever else it may be doing. In horses and dogs as well, that attentiveness is a valuable training asset in itself.

Because of the split-second timing that the conditioned reinforcer makes possible, the whistle also communicates just exactly what it is that the trainer is looking for. This allows you to teach the animal what you want, in a very clear way, one detail at a time. For example, let's say that a dolphin has assimilated one rule ("Jump facing this way"), and you know that because the animal almost always jumps with the proper orientation when you signal it to jump. Now you can add another detail or rule. You decide "I'll only reinforce the higher jumps." Pretty soon the dolphin has learned one more detail ("I have to jump facing this way and jump this high.")

This step-by-step process may seem elaborate, but in practice it is a fantastic shortcut to complex trained behavior. Even with a naive dolphin, a trainer can develop an on-cue, spectacular, and very specific behavior, such as the bow I've described, in two or three days—sometimes, if things go well, in a single 10-minute training session. Many times in my dolphin training experience I have "captured" a behavior, shaped it into something special, and put it on cue in a single training session; and so have other dolphin trainers.

HOW ABOUT DOGS?

You can easily experience dolphin-training your own dog, using a conditioned reinforcer, in one quick 10-minute experiment. Some dogs are afraid of whistles. A handy conditioned reinforcer for dogs is a clicker, a child's toy that goes click-click when you pinch it. They are available in toy and novelty shops, and some import stores.

Get yourself a clicker and a few treats. Make the treats small enough so that you can give the dog 15 or 20 treats without him filling up. Some dogs will work for kibble, especially just before dinnertime, but you might have to go to something more tempting in demonstrating this with strange dogs. I generally use diced chicken. Teach the dog the meaning of the click by clicking the clicker and giving a treat, four or five times, in different parts of the room or yard (so the dog doesn't get any funny ideas that this only works in one place).

Then click the clicker and delay the treat a few seconds; if you see the dog startle and actively look for the treat, you will know the signal has become a conditioned reinforcer. Now you can establish a behavior—we call this "shaping."

An easy behavior to shape is "chase your tail." There are, of course, as many ways to elicit this behavior as there are trainers to think them up: you could turn the dog around by its collar; you could put bacon grease on its tail tip so the dog circles to lick its tail. Here's one way to shape the behavior "from scratch," without any prompting.

Stop clicking and just wait. Your dog may be intrigued and excited by now; when you do nothing, the dog is likely to move around, and maybe even to whine and bark. The instant the dog happens to move or turn to the right, click your clicker. Give the treat.

Wait again. Ignore everything the dog does, except moving to the right (don't hold out for miracles; one turn of the head or one sideways step with the right front paw is all you need.) If you "catch" the behavior—if your timing is good—in three or four reinforcements you will see your dog turning to the right further and more often. Now you will find you don't need to reinforce just a single step to the right, but can reinforce right turns that go several steps, perhaps through a quarter of a circle; and, from a quarter turn, a full circle may come very quickly.

That's a good time to stop the first session: quit while you're ahead is the golden rule. Put the clicker away, with lots of hugs and praise, and try again the next day, starting with a single step, then a quarter circle, and then more; it will come much faster the second time.

From one circle, the next step is to get two circles, and the next step—an important one—is to go for a variety, rewarding half a circle sometimes, then two circles, or one, or three full turns, or just one and a quarter; this keeps the dog guessing. The click might come after one turn, or two, the dog doesn't know, so he keeps turning faster and faster; and thus you begin to develop an amusing whirl after his own tail.

This is a silly trick, of course, and not very dignified; there are other behaviors you could use for practice, such as targeting, in which you shape the animal to touch some object with its nose (sea lion trainers teach their animals to "target" on the trainer's closed fist; then by holding their fist on the ground or in the air or over a stand, they can move the sea lion where they want, without using force). The purpose of this experiment is not to teach the dog the trick, but to show you how to use a conditioned reinforcer to shape behavior and how effective this kind of reinforcement can be.

Why do you need to use a clicker? Why couldn't you just use your voice and the words "Good boy" as the conditioned reinforcer? The main reason is that you can't say a word, even "Good boy," with the split-second precision that you can achieve with a click. With the clicker and a little practice you can reinforce very tiny movements—one paw stepping to the right—in the instant that it occurs; a praise word is inevitably rather "fuzzy," because it takes longer.

The second difficulty with using a word is that we also talk near our dogs and even to our dogs when we are not reinforcing them. It is hard for the dog to sort the meaningful words out from the stream of noise we make, but the clicker is unlike any other sound in the room, and its meaning is crystal clear. You will in fact see the difference very clearly in the way the conditioned dog responds to the clicker (electric attention, galvanized, thrilled) as compared to the way the dog responds to "Good dog!" (Huh? Oh. Smile, wag.)

"Well," I've heard dog trainers say, "the clicker's good for tricks but not for anything else—you can't, for example, use it in the obedience ring." Of course not, and you don't need to. The clicker's value is in shaping new behavior, or refining details; it's not necessary in exhibiting behavior the animal has already learned. But even in the accomplished champion working dog, the conditioned reinforcer can be a useful training tool. One competitor told me he taught his Doberman to understand the clicker, and then used it to reinforce her for looking into his face, instead of away from him, while she worked. "It's as if she were grateful for the information, really: it cleared up the vagueness, for her," he said. Of course once the dog had come to understand what was wanted, she did correctly in the ring, without any clicks.

Don't think, however, that people never use a conditioned reinforcer in the ring; all the trainer has to do is establish a signal the dog is aware of that no one else notices. I know a keen obedience trainer who uses a barely audible sniff as a conditioned reinforcer. I have seen a competitor convey "Great job!" (as evinced by the overjoyed expression on the dog's face) just by touching one finger to her dog's head.

One competitor I know has taught her dog, Rex, that treats are called "Billy." Then as the dog performs in the obedience ring, she can reinforce an especially good behavior—a nice recall perhaps—with what appears to be a command: "Billy, heel!" No one questions why she doesn't use the dog's usual name in the ring.

Once a behavior is learned, there's no rule that says you have to give a tidbit for every click; so using a conditioned reinforcer allows you not only to delay the food, without loss to the performance, but to give less food overall; you don't have to worry that your animal will fill up before the job is done. One example: at dog shows I have often noticed handlers repeatedly baiting or feeding a dog to get nice pose or alert look. Whenever I see that food-food-food going down the dog's throat I know at once the person doesn't understand conditioned reinforcers! How much more effective it would be to "shape" the pose, develop a cue ("Ten-shun!") and then reinforce the dog with a click for assuming and holding the proper posture a respectable length of time, with the food later, outside the ring or when the judge has moved on.

Another virtue of the conditioned reinforcer is that it works—it conveys information and affects the animal's behavior—in all kinds of situations in which real reinforcement is not merely undesirable but in fact impossible. Think for example of how useful a simple conditioned reinforcer would be in training scent discriminations, tracking, long sits and downs, go-outs, pointing and flushing birds, and all other dog behaviors that require the animal to work away from you.

CONTROLLING MISBEHAVIOR WITH POSITIVE REINFORCEMENT

It might seem unreasonable that you can control bad behavior with positive reinforcement instead of "correction," but dolphin trainers have many ways to do it. Here are three examples:

- Establish a conditioned negative reinforcer: this does not need to be a signal that means, "I'm going to beat you" (although you could establish that, too) but a signal that means, "Nope, I'm not going to reinforce you." It tells the animal that some particular effort it is making is not going to pay off; the animal swiftly learns that whenever it gets this "red light" or "Wrong" signal it should change what it is doing. You could use such a signal, for example, to help teach a dog not to jump up in greeting, but to keep its paws on the floor for a patting reinforcement.

- Use positive reinforcement to train an incompatible behavior: in our dolphin shows at Sea Life Park, one animal took to harassing the girl swimmer who performed in the show. Rather than give the swimmer a stun gun (or some such punishment) we trained the dolphin to push on an underwater lever, for a whistle and fish, and we asked the animal to do that when the swimmer was in the water. The dolphin could not press its level and pester the swimmer at the same time; the behaviors are incompatible (and apparently lever-pressing was more reinforcing, because the swimmer harassment ceased). You are using this technique if you teach your dogs to lie in the doorway, at mealtimes, so they can't beg at the table.
- The time-out: sometimes a dolphin does something really bad, such as showing aggression (swinging its head or teeth at the trainer's hand, for example). The instant this happens, you turn your back, snatch up your training props and fish bucket, and leave, for one full minute. That's the end of all the fun. The dolphin is apt to stick its head out of the water looking dismayed—"Hey, what'd I do?" In a few repetitions it learns to mind its manners.

Time-outs are used successfully by oceanarium trainers to eliminate aggression toward human swimmers, even in highly dominant animals such as adult male killer whales, and to control many other sorts of misbehavior; the technique is, however, distressing to the animals and must be used sparingly. (The use of reinforcement to reduce misbehavior is discussed more fully in my books on training.)

MENTAL ATTITUDES

Using reinforcement is a lot of work for the trainer, because it forces you to think. Oh no, what pain! It's so much easier just to follow someone else's rules: if the dog makes a mess, rub his nose in it. If the dog doesn't heel, jerk the chain. However, in thinking about what you're going to reinforce, you'll be a better trainer. And the focus you will need, in order to perfect the timing of your reinforcements, makes training a thrill instead of a bore.

From the animal's standpoint, this kind of training is not a matter of learning how to stay out of trouble by doing what's required—a chore and nothing more. Instead, this kind of training gives the animal a chance to win, over and over, and also a chance to control at least part of its world. For example, from a dolphin's standpoint, once it has learned the meaning of the whistle, the training is not an exchange of commands and obedience, but a guessing game in which the dolphin tries to "discover" various ways to make the trainer blow that whistle. It is a game, with strict rules, but with equality on both sides. No wonder the dolphins enjoy their obedient trainers!

The effect of using the conditioned positive reinforcement is far more powerful than merely giving free goodies could ever be. If you stop relying on control of misbehavior and start shaping good behavior with clear-cut conditioned signals for reinforcement, your dog will respect you in a new way; to your dog, you will finally be making sense.

READING THE DOG

Before beginning training the handler needs to learn to recognize how his or her dog indicates changes in its environment through changes in body language. The dog cannot verbalize what it is sensing; however, it will send definite signals. Some signals may be subtle, but they can constitute a distinctive message to the handler with experience. These signals provide information that allows the handler to assess the work of the dog. Table 3.1 summarizes the changes in body language by which a dog may indicate scent changes in the environment to its handler.

Table 3.1 Canine Body Language Indicating Scent Changes in the Environment

A. Head position	A level head with little air exchange generally means the dog is using eyesight and is not using its nose. The head held high in the air accompanied by nasal exchange indicates the dog is air scenting. The head down while the canine continues at a normal gait normally indicates the dog is tracking/ trailing If the dog stops and sniffs at one spot, then urinates, the dog may be marking over an animal odor. If it paws the ground and becomes animated, it may be working the scent source. As the handler progresses in training, he or she can normally tell when the dog smells an animal odor.
B. Ears	With prick-eared dogs, the ears may come forward when the dog nears a scent source.

C. Eyes	A free-ranging dog commonly will stop and make direct eye contact with the handler. The contact will be obvious; then the dog will proceed to the scent source.
D. Tail	The tail is one of the most expressive parts of the dog's anatomy. The dog will carry its tail in a certain configuration during the search. When it encounters the scent cone, the tail may rise, or it may drop, but normally it will begin to wag rapidly as the animal nears the source.
E. Hackles	The dog may raise its hackles as it nears the source.
F. Circling	This action may mean several things. The dog may be in a scent pool and attempting to work it out. The subject may be in a tree. The area may have scent carried by a thermal lift and there is no cone for the dog to work.
G. Breathing	The dog's respiration increases rapidly indicating a change in the scent picture. It usually occurs when the dog is close to the source. Known as "shutting down," the breaths become stacked, and, if the handler pays attention, he or she can both see and hear it happening.
H. Overall Attitude Change	The dog's whole demeanor changes, indicating that it perceives a radical change in the working environment. Most dogs become extremely animated as they work closer to the source. Occasionally a dog will become subdued. Once it reaches the source it should perform its trained indication or alert.

Each dog is an individual and reacts differently. During training, the handler must observe the dog closely and analyze how this particular dog reacts to the entire spectrum of scent in a variety of search circumstances. The ability to "read" the dog reliably will take time, but will prove invaluable in the future.

Training Principles

by Marcia Koenig

In *A Dog and a Dolphin,* excerpted earlier, Karen Pryor describes training using positive reinforcement and a conditioned reinforcer. In the following discussion those concepts will be applied to scent dog training.

CLICKER

The clicker is a small hand-held, portable device that can be used to signal the dog that, "You're doing the right thing! The reward is coming!" A word can also work, but a word is not as unique a sound as a clicker. Once the dog knows the click means the reward is coming, you can use it to tell the dog that it has done the right thing.

Use the clicker when you are imprinting the cadaver scent. When the dog hears the "click" it begins to understand that this scent is something you want it to remember. Dogs who are given a signal when they are doing the right thing learn faster and are more accurate at pinpointing scents. We have done studies in dog training classes comparing training with the clicker and without it. Particularly when training for a buried scent source, dogs that are signaled "That's right!" with a click when their noses are right over the source become more precise in their indications of buried scent. Many dogs will touch the exact area with their noses.

REWARDS

Training the dog to find people, alive or dead, is simply a modification of instinctive hunting behavior. Instead of getting to kill the prey, the dog gets a reward from the handler. This reward can be anything the dog wants: food, play, or the opportunity to do a favorite behavior (such as swimming). The more the dog wants the reward, the more intense its search behavior will be.

It is your job as trainer to find things that turn your dog on. Experiment and let the dog "tell" you what it likes. For example, I was demonstrating how to shape following my hand with a young labrador retriever. The owner had given me some dry dog biscuits. The dog had very little interest in my hand. It paid more attention to the other dog smells on the stage. I asked if anyone had more interesting food and was given a stick of fish sausage (I was in Japan). When the lab smelled the fish sausage, I immediately had its complete attention. Learning goes much faster if the dog thinks the reward is wonderful! And if you have a number of different rewards, the search game will remain interesting.

PHASES OF LEARNING[1]

Teaching

1. **Break the behavior you want to train into small steps.** With each step the dog should have better than a 50% chance of doing it correctly. If the dog is not succeeding, break the behavior down even further. This decreases frustration for both the dog and handler.
2. **Train one thing at a time.** Dogs learn faster when they only have one thing to learn at a time. For example, imprint the scent (see below) as a separate exercise without having the dog search for the scent. You can train for more than one thing at a time, but it will take longer than training each separately and putting the two together.
3. **End problems successfully.** If the problem is not going well, do what you need to end it successfully. Or end the training on a simpler motivational problem.
4. **Chain steps backward.** When you train the last part of a behavior chain first, the dog is always going from something it's unfamiliar with to something it knows very well.[2] For example, many dog handlers want their dog to take them back to the scent source. The steps for training begin with the last item in the search problem sequence (see Table 3.2). If the dog has a problem at any of these steps, break it down into smaller pieces.
5. **Lower criteria or simplify training when in a new area.** Many times a handler in our classes will say, "I don't know what's wrong. My dog knows how to do this behavior. He does it perfectly at home." But the dog is not at home. Any time the dog is in an unfamiliar place, behavior will deteriorate. Lower your expectations and the behavior will soon be up to its usual level.

Developing Fluency

Fluency is defined as doing the behavior quickly and accurately. If you can type 120 words per minute, but have 5 errors, you are not fluent in typing. Or if you can type with zero errors, but only at 35 words per minute, you are still not fluent in typing. You must be both fast and accurate. How do you get there? Practice, practice, practice. The same is true in dog training. To have a dog that is fluent in cadaver

[1] Adapted from Marcia Koenig and Tom Osterkamp, ©1998.

[2] This works well with children too, especially practicing for piano recitals. If the child is taught the last section of the musical piece first, then the middle, then the beginning, she will be going from less familiar music to more familiar music. Her confidence will increase as she continues playing.

work requires many, many repetitions. If you dog is not both fast and accurate, you need more practice.

Ensuring Automatic Response

Dogs are very poor at generalization. For example, if you teach your dog to "sit" in front of you, you will also need to teach the dog to "sit" beside you. If the dog is taught "sit" inside your house, it will also need to be taught "sit" outside. And if it sits outside next to you, it will need to be taught "sit" away from you.

What this means is that you will need to teach your dog to find cadaver scent everywhere you can think of. The more different experiences a dog has, the more it will be able to generalize to new experiences. As the dog gains confidence, add distractions. Lower your criteria when you add distractions as it will take time and experience for the dog to learn to ignore distractions.

Maintenance

Maintain the skills by practicing at least twice a month, or more frequently.

Problems

If you are having training problems, back up to where the dog was successful. It won't take long to get back to where you were. In order to do advanced training, the dog must have a good foundation in basic scent work. Finally, it never hurts to do refresher training periodically . This will sharpen the dogs' skills and increase reliability.

Table 3.2 Comparison of Problem Sequence with Teaching Order

Search Problem Sequence		Teaching Order
1. Command to locate—"Find bones."	Step 1	Take handler to body
2. Come back to handler	Step 2	Bark at handler Take handler to body
3. Bark at handler	Step 3	Come back to handler Bark at handler Take handler to body
4. Take handler to body	Step 4	Command to locate Come back to handler Bark at handler Take handler to body

TRAINING PROGRESSION

The purpose of any training exercise is to build the handler's confidence in the ability of the dog to locate a desired scent source and to reinforce the dog for its performance. To realize maximum benefits, training exercises must be set up as realistically as possible. It can duplicate an actual search in which the unit has participated or can be tailored to a specific training site.

Cadaver scent work is taught in a step-wise progression. This step-by-step procedure insures that both the handler and dog are competent at each level before proceeding to more difficult problems. The first steps establish a solid foundation of scent recognition. Next steps build on that foundation until the dog can reliably cover a large area and correctly indicate the location of the scent source with a *trained indication (alert)*.

All of these steps are mechanical and should be taught under controlled conditions. Each step requires multiple repetitions in order to build a solid foundation for the next. Once the dog becomes proficient at one stage, the trainer can begin the next. However, trainers must remember to drop or soften their criteria when moving to the next phase. If the animal falters, drop back to the previous step.

Progressive specialty training includes the specific phases itemized below. At the beginning of each step, the handler should be aware of the location of the scent source. (Note: Please see the section on Training Equipment in Chapter 4, Materials, for an overview of items and set-up needed for the following phases.)

PHASE I — IMPRINTING

This phase focuses on scent recognition and commitment to the target odor, or *imprinting*. It includes seven steps. The target scent is introduced to the dog, and the dog is rewarded for recognizing this scent differentiated from others. As the dog learns to differentiate, that response is strengthened by repetition until there is a definite commitment to the scent.

Once commitment is established, a set of secondary stimuli are introduced which the dog is taught to associate with the scent commitment. This may include putting a specific collar or harness on the dog as well as verbal cues or commands to find the target odor, which are repeated each time the exercise is performed.

By the end of this phase the following sequence and skills are in place:

- The cues that this is a search (e.g., put on special collar) are provided.
- The command/cue is given (e.g.,"Find it").

- When the dog indicates with its secondary alert that it has entered a scent cone, a reward is given.
- When it finds the target odor source and gives its primary alert, it is immediately rewarded.

It is important that each of *the cues are specific for this particular behavioral sequence,* for example, the search situation cue (special collar), the specific command ("find it"—not used in other situations), and the specific reward (special treat or special toy).

The Trained Indication (Alert)

A special behavior by the dog is chosen to be its *trained alert*. This is the trained indication the dog gives when it finds the scent. Generally, a behavior is chosen which comes naturally to that particular dog when it is presented with the target odor. Then, when the indication behavior is chosen, the handler consistently cues that action when the dog indicates the target odor. The dog must receive an immediate and consistent reward when the target odor is indicated. This reward will be both verbal and include something valuable to that particular dog (e.g., a treat or a toy). And the reward must be *given at the source,* to give the impression to the dog that the reward actually comes directly from the target odor source location.

The dog's natural behavior in response to contact with the target odor should be carefully noted. This behavior, termed the *natural alert*, will be a cue to the handler that the dog has located the scent. When the handler observes the secondary alert, indicating the dog has entered a scent cone or pool, immediate, secondary reinforcement will encourage the dog to work to locate the source. The secondary reinforcement should be different from that given for locating the actual target source.

Step 1: Scent Introduction — Teach target scent recognition

At first, the exercise should be done on lead. Timing of reward is crucial, since you are attempting to teach the dog to recognize a new target odor. If using a clicker, you will click when the dog shows the slightest interest in the block with the source. If using verbal praise, time the reinforcement word as soon as the dog shows the slightest indication that it detects a different odor. Remember to give the reward close to the source. If you are using food, hold the piece right over the hole of the block. If using a toy (ball or Kong™), make it appear that it popped out of the hole. These principles hold true for all training.

Procedure

With the dog on lead, start down the line of blocks, or *scent line* (see Chapter 4 for set-up details). The dog probably will be ahead of you, so watch the dog for the slightest indication that it has perceived a different odor. If the dog stops and drops its nose to the block, reward it immediately. If the dog proceeds down the line without showing any indication, do not become alarmed. Start again at the first block and keep the dog closer to you, targeting each block as you proceed. When you reach the *hot block*, the dog may check it when you target it; reward as soon as it drops its head towards the source.

Work the line two or three times, rewarding the dog each time it indicates the source. Then start from the other end so that the source is now in a different position. Work the dog as before, rewarding at the slightest indication and, when you get to the other end, turn around and work back. Using this method the dog is exposed to the scent twice in one rotation.

Once you have exposed the dog to the source 10–15 times, give it a break. A good play period will help keep the dog well motivated.

Before beginning another rotation, either add more blocks to the line or change the hot block to a different position. Make sure you move both the block and the container. Otherwise you will have a block with residual scent and no source. The dog will probably indicate the block. If not rewarded (and many handlers do not reward if they cannot see the source) the dog may ignore the real source when it reaches it.

During these exercises, do not expect anything more than the dog indicating the source by dropping its head and sniffing deeply. You are simply teaching the dog to recognize the target scent.

Before proceeding, you should repeat the rotation two or three times (30–45 exposures to the scent).

Step 2: Develop *Scent Commitment* — Strengthen scent recognition

Procedure

Set up a line of blocks as before. The source initially should be in the fourth or fifth block. With the dog on leash, start down the line, watching the animal carefully for it to indicate the hot block. As soon as it drops its head to the source, remain quiet and when it lifts its head, ask it to *"show me."* The dog should again drop its nose to the source. As soon as it does, *click and treat.* Make sure to give the reward at the source.

Repeat the exercise several times working from both ends of the line. After 10 repetitions, give the dog a play break. Breaks should come immediately after the dog has done a good indication. The dog will consider it a "jackpot" earned by its performance.

Repeat this exercise, however, set up another jar with Pseudo™ Corpse Formulation II. Add the second source to the block line-up, so there are two targets for the dog to indicate. Make sure you click and treat at each indication. When the dog is reliable at showing you the target on the cue "show me," you are ready to proceed to the next step. Make sure that you have done 30–45 repetitions at this step.

Step 3: Introduce the Command (Cue) — Cue each task

In most cases, you will have a *cue* for each search task. For example, the air-scent area search dog responds to cue when its *search vest* is put on and it is given the verbal cue "go search." A tracking/trailing dog is taken to the area where it is to start, put in a trailing harness and given the verbal cue "track" or "find 'em." Multi-task dogs need a cue for each task. For example, a patrol dog that does handler protection, building search, article search, and tracking would have a different verbal cue for each task. In this case they might be "get 'em" for handler protection, "search 'em out" for building search, "seek" for article search, and "find 'em" for tracking. In addition, the handler might use a special collar for aggression work and a tracking harness in conjunction with the verbal cue for tracking.

Your approach to selecting a cue for cadaver search will depend on what type of search you plan to work. If your primary mission is wilderness search for live persons and you simply wish to introduce the dog to cadaver scent so it will indicate the subject if deceased, you may decide to use the same cue as you use for live search. Your training would then emphasize that the dog responds to both live and deceased scent in the search area.

If you are training cadaver search as a primary task, then you need to select a specific word to use as a cue. Some examples are: "find Fred," "bones," "find Mort," and "look." Pick a word that is not going to embarrass you if you need to start the dog on a search and the news media or family members are in the immediate area.

The command will be used to cue the dog each time you start an exercise. If you so desire, you can also use a special collar or harness as a signal that the dog is to look for human remains. However, in some areas, especially if in heavy brush, it is not a good idea to leave a collar or harness on the animal if it is to range a long distance. It may become entangled.

When you first introduce the cue, use an excited voice and encourage the dog. Remember that until the dog associates the word with the scent source, it hasn't the foggiest idea what you want. You need to make the association between the cue and the scent. This will take a number of repetitions.

Procedure

With the dog on leash, start at the line of blocks. Give the cue in an excited voice. Work the dog along the line, and when it indicates the hot block, reward immediately. In this case you are not going to ask the dog to "show me." Since it is a new exercise, we need to drop our criteria until the dog associates the cue with the task. Then we will work to build a stronger commitment.

Repeat the exercise several times, then move the scent source. After 10-15 repetitions you should begin to get cue association from the animal. Make sure you give a play break after finishing the exercise.

Step 4: Introduce the Trained Indication (Alert)

The *trained alert* is the indication that the dog is trained to perform when it encounters the target odor. The handler can either capitalize on a natural reaction that the animal has demonstrated when it was working the imprinting problems or the handler can pick a specific action for the dog to perform. This *trained indication* can be either active or passive. Many law enforcement agencies prefer a passive alert to prevent disturbance of a crime scene where an active alert may disturb the area.

Examples of types of indications are:

- Active—digging; barking
- Passive—sitting; lying down

Once you select a behavior, stick with it. Nothing confuses a dog more than the handler changing the parameters during training.

The trained alert must be consistently repeatable, and the handler must be able to articulate the dog's indication to others. You may be asked "How does your dog indicate when he finds a body?" You must be able to describe the reaction.

If you have noticed that your dog shows a specific behavior when working the scent in the previous steps, it will make it easy to teach the trained alert. With my young dog, as we proceeded through the imprinting stage working on a loose lead, I noted that he began to sit each time he checked the hot block. When it was time to teach his indication, it went very rapidly since I utilized the sitting behavior that occurred naturally on his part.

In order for the behavior to become consistent, do not rush this step. As you proceed through the next phases of training, insist on the trained indication in each exercise. If the dog becomes sloppy, do not hesitate to cue the behavior. In some cases it may become necessary to go back to some very basic exercises to reinforce the alert.

Later, some dogs may be trained to give an indication they have found a target at a distant location. The handler then directs the dog to take him or her there; this is called a *refind.* It will be taught as a separate exercise after the dog becomes fluent on performing its final, trained alert.

Procedure

With the dog on leash, give the dog its cue and start along the line of blocks. When the dog indicates the hot block by dipping its head or pawing, ask it to "show me." As soon as the dog confirms that the target scent is in the block, cue its trained indication.

A repetition using sitting as a trained indication should go something like this:

1. "Find Fred"
2. Work down the line
3. Dog puts nose deep into the block and lifts head out, makes eye contact with the handler
4. "Show me" (light and excited)
5. Dog again puts nose deep into the block
6. "Sit"
7. As soon as the hind end hits the ground, the reward (food or toy) is given right at the top of the block
8. Handler gives effusive verbal praise and runs off to play with the dog for a few minutes before repeating the exercise.

Repeat the exercise 10–15 times, then give the dog a break. Then repeat for another rotation of 10–15 repetitions.

After a couple of sessions the trained alert will begin to occur automatically. Then you should employ the "rule of 10." Work the scent line and when the dog indicates the hot block, ask it to "show me." The dog should again indicate the block. Now you wait for the behavior to occur naturally. Once the dog has confirmed, start to count to 10 silently. This gives the dog 10–15 seconds to perform the trained alert on its own. If the behavior does not occur, once you finish the count, immediately cue it. Make sure you reward immediately when the dog alerts.

If the behavior breaks down, don't be afraid to back up and start over with very basic exercises. The dog learns through repetition and being amply rewarded when it performs as expected.

Step 5: Introduce Additional Target Odors

The cadaver dog must be trained to respond to a wide spectrum of scent, from recently deceased to skeletal remains that have been in the environment or buried for many years. Each stage of decomposition presents a different scent picture. Once the animal is responding well during initial imprinting, we introduce other odors using the same method. Remember, drop your expectations and initially reward the dog for the slightest indication to the new scent source.

Procedure

Expand the block setup. Either use two lines of six blocks or a large circle with all twelve blocks. Make sure that when you remove a scent source from a block, either remove the block from the line or place a different source in the hot block.

For the first few rotations, use the initial source (Pseudo™ Corpse Formulation II) in one block and the new source in another one. Make sure there are some negative blocks between the sources. Start the dog at a position where it will detect the already imprinted scent first. Reward upon indication. Start the dog again; this time, watch for a reaction when it reaches the new source. As soon as it dips its head towards the target, "click and treat." Continue the exercise until the dog has worked the two sources for a total of 10 indications.

After a break, work the exercise again; however, this time you can ask the dog to "show me" at the new target. After a few repetitions, you may be able to move on to having the dog do its trained indication on the new source. Make sure you cue it the first few times, then employ the rule of 10 to see if the dog will react automatically.

There is a big advantage to placing the blocks in a circle. You can vary the starting point so that the dog doesn't begin to anticipate the exact location of the source.

By now, you should be able to work the dog on a loose lead. Work the circle after giving the verbal cue, walking at a steady pace. Do not slow down or stop when you reach the hot block. If the dog passes the block, give it the opportunity to turn around and return to the source and alert. Reward immediately!

Repeat this exercise with other sources, i.e., soil, dried blood, or decomposition odor. Make sure the dog has become reliable with its trained alert and rarely needs to be cued.

Step 6: Working Off Lead

Once the dog is consistently showing good odor recognition and indicating as trained, then you should work several repetitions with the dog off lead. Remember, this is a new situation for the animal, so make sure you reinforce at the various stages of scent recognition. If you are using a clicker, and have moved to using it to mark desired behavior, you can use the clicker to mark each step: recognition, commitment, and alert. If not, when the dog stops at the hot block and indicates it has scent, give it the "show me" cue, let it re-indicate the source, and then cue it to alert. As soon as it performs its trained alert, run up and amply reward it.

You will need to work 10–15 repetitions so the dog becomes comfortable working away from you and will begin to indicate on its own. Make sure the dog is given ample reward, an occasional jackpot when it does an exemplary job, and breaks between exercises.

Step 7: Introducing the Refind if Desired

Many handlers doing air scent area search teach the dog to come back to them, perform some action and, on cue, take the handler back to the subject: the *refind*. This is a very reliable indication, especially when the dog is ranging a good distance. Since many cadaver searches are conducted in limited areas, it is not necessary to teach the refind. If you do elect to do so, the dog must first be firm on its commitment to the scent source and performing a reliable trained indication.

I have traditionally taught my dogs to do a refind, touching a toy on my belt or a ball in my jacket pocket, then taking me directly back to the source, and performing their alert as close to the source as possible. My refind also worked for water search in a boat. When the dog detected scent, it would nudge the toy then indicate by sitting or downing in the boat.

There are two methods of teaching the refind to a scent source.

Procedure 1

With the dog on lead, work along a line of blocks. When the dog locates the hot block, let the leash go slack as the dog commits to the source. Back up the length of the leash without putting pressure on it. When the dog makes eye contact with you, call it. When it gets back to you, cue it to touch the toy and then ask "show me." The dog should turn and head back to the source. Move fast, and when you get to the block, cue the dog to do its trained alert. Work this method a few times and then try it with the dog off leash. Remember, drop your criteria. Just because the dog knows the refind for another task does not mean it will immediately translate to desired behavior for the new task. The behavior should begin to occur reliably after a dozen or so repetitions.

Procedure 2

With the dog off lead, give the search cue and send it to work the line of blocks. Watch for the indication that it has located the source. As soon as it makes a commitment, call it. When it returns to you, cue the desired indication. As soon as the dog makes the indication, ask it to "show me" and run excitedly to the source. When it reaches the source, immediately cue it to perform the trained primary indication and then enthusiastically reward.

Both these methods require many repetitions to make the behavior occur automatically. The whole object is to have the animal perform the desired behavior any time it encounters one of the imprinted odors.

All of the above are mechanical operations and are taught under controlled conditions. Each step requires multiple repetitions in order to build a solid foundation for scent indication. Once the animal becomes proficient at a step, the trainer can begin the next step. However, the trainer must remember to drop his or her criteria when moving to the next phase. If the animal falters, drop back to the previous step.

PHASE II—SMALL AREA SEARCH WITH HIDDEN SOURCE

Once recognition, commitment, and indication (alert) are established in response to the search command, and the reinforcing cues are reliably associated with the behavior, the dog is next taught to search for a *hidden source* in a relatively small area. The source is hidden from view in a portable object such as a concrete block and the dog is taken through the search command/find/alert/reward sequence. This sequence skill is reliably established, and then the task is varied slightly. For example, the location might be varied, or the source might be placed in a different sort of location (e.g., under some small logs).

When the handler is confident of the dog's ability to detect the desired scent, and he or she can read the alert reliably, then the exercise is performed with the handler not knowing the location of the source. Now the handler has to learn to believe the dog when it alerts. The handler should be accompanied by a trainer during this set of "blind" problems. This is to assure that the handler does not inadvertently reinforce a false alert. It is only human nature to encourage the dog if it should show interest in an area, but reinforcing a false alert would compromise the training process.

In fact there are many odors that may interest the dog, e.g., animal urine, possible decomposed animal matter, etc. The handler must be able to recognize the difference between a general interest in an area and the more intense interest in the target source.

In this phase, you will be teaching the dog to search a small area without a visible target. The handler should observe the dog's body language carefully for an indication that it has detected the target odor and reinforce it as soon as it locates the source.

Procedure

- Select a grassy or wooded area approximately 20 yards square. Make sure you can observe the dog when it is working. Throw a scent tube into the area in a place where it will be concealed from view and wait 15-30 minutes. This will allow a scent cone to form.
- Approach the area from downwind. Give the dog its search cue and watch it carefully as it works the area. If necessary, begin to walk a *grid pattern* so the animal thoroughly covers the area. That

is, walk in parallel paths about 10–12 feet wide, perpendicular to the wind, gradually moving nearer to the target (see also Chapter 11). When the dog's body language indicates that it has detected the scent, encourage it to work to the source. As soon as the dog's nose drops to the source, use your secondary reinforcer (verbal or clicker) and cue the dog to perform its primary trained indication. Then enthusiastically reward the dog.

- In another area, set up a similar problem and start the dog. With several repetitions it will soon realize that it is to search the area and indicate the source. Stay back and when the dog pinpoints the tube, begin your count in order to give the dog time to perform the trained alert on its own. If you finish your count and the dog has not done its trained indication, cue it. Then reward.

As you proceed, the trained indication (alert) will begin to occur naturally. Remember that the purpose is to make the dog's indication consistent and repeatable under all types of conditions.

PHASE III—SMALL AREA SEARCH FOR A BURIED SOURCE

Once the handler and dog are proficient in locating a hidden source in a small area, the target odor is hidden by burying it.

The initial (natural) alert, especially for a *buried source*, may be very subtle. If the source has been in that location a long time, it may create a fairly strong scent pool in the general area. The dog may work the pool and set the perimeter, but will have difficulty working directly into the source.

If this occurs during the free search of the area, note the boundaries the dog has indicated. The dog should receive secondary reinforcement for the response to the scent pool perimeter, which will encourage it to go directly to the source (for the primary reinforcement). If the dog still has a problem, check wind direction and adjust the search tactics to a closer, more directed grid search (see Chapter 8 for a discussion of grid searches) within the area. With proper technique, the dog should eventually be able to go directly to the source.

The initial search areas for buried problems should be kept small. Search for buried items is extremely intense for the dog and it requires maximum reinforcement, even though both the natural and trained alerts may initially be very subtle.

Buried problems should be set up a minimum of 6 hours in advance to give scent time to migrate to the surface and form a cone. If working in tightly compacted soils, the problem should be set at least 24 hours in advance.

The trainer should dig the soil at several locations. This will acclimate the dog to the odor of disturbed earth, and prevent the dog from a false alert when no cadaver odor is present. The site itself should show as little disturbance as possible, and the gravesite can be camouflaged. As training progresses, sites can be selected that contain animal decomposition to act as a distraction to the dog.

Search for a buried source is a normal expansion from looking for a concealed surface source. Initially the dog may have trouble realizing that the odor originates from under ground. Again, drop your criteria when you begin the exercises, however, it will not take many repetitions for the animal to grasp the concept.

Procedure

- Select an area approximately 10 yards by 10 yards preferably with gravel or a light loam soil. For the first few repetitions, bury the source 4–8 inches deep. Dig several negative holes in the same area. The negative holes will help insure that the dog is not indicating just to disturbed soil. Wait a minimum of 30 minutes to allow a scent cone to form.
- You may want to work the dog on lead for the first time.This will allow you to control the search pattern. Many dogs have an inclination to work the area too fast and have problems detecting the odor.
- Start the dog *quartering the wind*. That is, move perpendicular to the wind direction. When the dog gives its initial indication that it has detected the odor, encourage it to pinpoint. Once it's nose drops to the proper hole, cue the desired alert.

You can use the same area for several problems. Simply start the dog from a different area each time. As it becomes more proficient in locating the buried source, wait the brief time before cueing the alert.

Change areas and set up problems that age longer before you work them. Here is where you will begin to see the dog work a scent pool prior to committing to the source. Let the dog work the pool, however, do not let it leave the area without pinpointing the source. You do not want the dog leaving a source once it has indicated that it has detected the target odor. However, it is very common for a dog to locate the source, check the immediate area, and then return to the proper location and indicate.

Once the dog has become proficient in locating the buried source, you can increase the burial depth, area size, and type of soil. If working in soil with a heavy clay composition, let the problem sit overnight before working. It takes much longer for the cone to form in the tighter soil. Since the majority of criminal burials are no deeper than two feet, it is not necessary to set up practice problems buried much deeper than 15-18 inches.

Make sure the dog is enthusiastically reinforced upon the completion of each problem.

PHASE IV—SMALL AREA SEARCH FOR A HANGING SUBJECT

Thus far, the emphasis has been on training the dog on surface or subsurface targets. Since you may be involved in a search for a subject that has committed suicide by hanging, the dog needs to be introduced to a suspended scent source. Initially, when the dog locates the area of the *hanging subject* source, it may circle or check the ground and not look up. Since the dog has indicated it has located the target, if it has a problem pinpointing its exact location, do not be afraid to target the source and reinforce the dog as soon as it indicates. Most dogs will jump up in an attempt to touch the source. This is a natural reaction regardless of its trained alert. Once it jumps up, it can be cued to perform the trained indication.

Procedure

- In a relatively open wooded area approximately 50 yards by 50 yards, place a scent tube in a tree about 6 feet from the ground. The tube can be hung or taped to a branch, but should not be immediately visible to the dog.
- Starting at the downwind perimeter, give the dog the search cue and let it work the area. Watch carefully for an indication that the dog has entered the scent cone. If the dog reaches the source and indicates that it is high by head action, jumping, or other behavior, use your secondary reinforcement and then cue the desired alert.
- If the dog works the cone and is concentrating on the ground, move in close to the source and verbally encourage the animal. If it acts confused, target the tube and immediately reinforce the dog. If the dog still acts confused, target the source by holding the toy near it. The dog will associate the high odor with the toy and should perform with more confidence during additional problems.
- You can then work another problem, cueing the desired alert when the dog indicates the source.

It is a good idea to work a surface problem shortly after the hanging session. The first time the animal will probably check up the trees in the immediate area of the source before locating it on the ground. This behavior is normal. Reward the dog immediately when it indicates the source.

One variation that provides a challenge is to hide the source next to a stream. The scent will channel downstream and stay close to the water. With practice, the dog will leave the water and go to the source.

PHASE V—LARGE AREA SEARCH FOR AN ABOVE-SURFACE SOURCE

Now that you have introduced the dog to locating a scent source under a variety of conditions, the time has come to widen the search area. The size of the search area should be increased gradually as handler confidence builds. Both handler and dog need to become comfortable with searching an area and working for a period of time before the dog locates the source. This phase gives you an opportunity to practice good search coverage techniques and allows you to train for systematic and logical search patterns.

Procedure

- Select a lightly wooded area between 5 and 10 acres. Place the scent source well concealed in the last one-third of the area to be covered. Let it sit for several hours or overnight.
- Start the dog on one boundary and use good tactics to cover the area thoroughly. When the dog gives an initial indication that it has located the scent cone, watch to see if it will work to the source. If the dog leaves the cone, bring it back into the area, and when it gives an initial indication, verbally encourage it to work out the problem.
- When it pinpoints the source, wait for the trained alert. If it is not performed by the time you finish your count, cue the dog.

Work several of these problems using different sources with a different placement, i.e., under a brush pile, in a drainage ditch, a hanging source. Use your imagination to set up the problem; however, you need to remember this is still a training exercise to improve the animal's performance, not an exercise to try to fool the dog.

A good air scent exercise is to place the target odor in brush or heavy grass on the fringe of a large open field so that the scent cone goes across the field. The dog will hit the cone at a distance, giving the handler an opportunity to watch the dog's actions and to properly reinforce it before it reaches the target.

Variations can be introduced by placing the material on the side of a hill, ravine, or gully. Normally the scent will pool either at the foot or top of the hill, depending on the time of day (see Chapter 2). There may be a thermal break in the scent cone, so the dog may be unable to work directly to the source. The handler is then challenged to analyze the alert with consideration of the terrain and change search tactics to complete the problem.

The trainer can set up a problem along a road, setting the scent material by throwing it from a vehicle. There will be no scent trail leading to the source. The handler is then given parameters for the general search area. This scenario duplicates many homicide cases, where the body is dumped along a road and the team has only general landmarks to use for search boundaries.

Occasionally the dog may alert in an area created by "thermal lift" of a scent from a remote location (see Chapter 2). This area should be marked and a secondary but no primary reinforcement given. After the dog/handler team has searched by cross-gridding an area without the dog locating the source, the team can return and re-search the "hot" area.

As the dog gains confidence, and with proper reinforcement on your part, you will see your desired trained alert become the normal pinpoint behavior for the dog.

PHASE VI—LARGE AREA SEARCH FOR A BURIED SOURCE

This exercise is an expansion of the initial buried search. The dog must do a systematic search of the area.

Procedure

- Select an area approximately 2 to 3 acres (100 yards by 100 yards). Your initial problems should be set up in an area with a fairly open soil type: gravel, sand, or loam.
- Bury the scent source 6–12 inches deep. Wait for several hours for a scent pool and cone to form. Dig several negative holes in the search area.
- Start the dog quartering the wind and control the search so it performs an *open grid search*. That is, keep the paths back and forth across the search area roughly perpendicular to the wind and roughly parallel to each other. Watch carefully for indications it has entered the scent area.
- Give the dog the opportunity to work to the source. It may work the pool several times. Do not let the dog indicate the area and then leave without giving its trained alert. Remember to reward at the source.

A good future exercise may be worked in the area if you leave the source buried, then return to work it again a week or more later. There will be a difference in the scent cone depending on the intervening environmental conditions, and it will provide valuable training for both you and the dog. Make sure you map the source location so you can locate it. We have left sources buried for several years. It is interesting to compare the dog's reactions with the early search and one done two or three years later.

PHASE VII —NEGATIVE AREA SEARCH

Many actual searches are speculative and have negative results. Such searches are often necessary to rule out an area; in these situations the absence of the dog's alert constitutes valuable information. Searches with no finds are frustrating to both dog and handler; however, the handler has to draw a conclusion after completing the area. During training, the team should search an area without a scent source, and praise the dog for its performance when done. They should then do a short, reinforcement problem with reward at the end to maintain the dog's proficiency and interest.

Procedure

- Pick an area where you have not previously trained with cadaver scent. This will prevent the dog from giving an indication on residual scent. Give the dog its cue and thoroughly work the area.
- Do not accept any trained indication from the dog. It is important if the dog shows interest that you not let it give a false alert.
- Once you have finished searching the negative area, reward the dog with a play period.
- When the dog has been rewarded for working a successful search, take it into a small area with a scent source. Cue the dog and let it work the new area. Reward its trained alert.

PHASE VIII—BLIND AREA SEARCH

In order to replicate actual search situations, training exercises should be set up in which the trainer, but not the handler, knows where the target material is hidden. In these situations, the handler's ability to assess the terrain, wind, and search parameters will be critically tested.

At this point in the training, the dog should be effectively searching an area and performing its trained alert when it locates the source. Prior to this, training should have been conducted with the handler having knowledge of the location of the source. In this way, he or she learns to evaluate the animal's reaction and cue the dog so the alert becomes solid.

Another handler should set up the blind problem. If possible, that handler should accompany you so that he or she can evaluate the work and, if the dog gives a false alert, advise you so you do not reward. The source may be surface covered, hanging, or buried. It should be placed sufficiently in advance so a scent cone develops. They should give you area boundaries to allow you to conduct an efficient search.

Once the dog indicates the location of a source, give it time to perform the trained alert. Then make sure that you reward at the source.

When you have worked several blind searches, you are ready for a formal evaluation.

PHASE IX—TEST

The test should be blind with regard to the handler. It should be as realistic as possible. And it should provide an adequate opportunity for the trainer to assess the behavior of both handler and dog.

Handler/team evaluations depend upon the requirements of their unit. Most units require a formal test and set specific requirements that must be met in order to be considered "mission ready." The test is set up to be as realistic as possible and run as if it were an actual search. The evaluation should not only consider whether the dog can indicate the scent source, but how the handler plans the search, how effectively the handler works the area, control of the dog, and whether the dog performs its trained alert appropriately. It is an automatic failure if the handler calls a false alert.

Evaluators may include other handlers or operational leaders from the handler's unit or handlers from outside your unit.

The requirements below were developed initially for law enforcement agencies and are used currently for all Specialty Search basic classes.

K-9 BASIC CADAVER SEARCH PROFICIENCY TEST

Purpose: To establish minimum standards of proficiency and reliability of dogs in the detection of human remains or parts thereof.

Needs: All canine teams shall demonstrate their proficiency in the search techniques used to locate bodies or parts of bodies either above, on or below the surface.

Scent Source: The scent source used may be a chemical simulating human decomposition (i.e., Sigma Pseudo™ Corpse Formulation I or II), soil samples from a grave, aged human blood or other suitable source. The source should be in a container to prevent the dog from making contact with it. There shall be a minimum of one and a maximum of two training aids used. If two sources are used, one must be above surface.

Search Area: The search will be conducted in an area one hundred (100) yards by one hundred (100) yards minimum. The area shall have moderate vegetation.

Time: The team will be allowed a maximum of one (1) hour to conduct the search.

Test: The training aid(s) shall be placed in the test area a minimum of twelve (12) hours prior to testing and shall be either above ground, (no higher than 6 feet), on the surface or buried no deeper than 12 inches below soil surface. Aboveground sources shall be concealed so as not to be immediately visible to the handler. The burial site shall be camouflaged so visible ground disturbance is minimal. There shall be a minimum of three holes dug to insure the dog does not alert on earth disturbance. If possible, there shall be animal remains as a distraction on the surface in the testing area.

Evaluation: All proficiency testing shall be done on a pass/fail basis. For certification, the team must pass the following:

- Locate all aids placed for testing.
- Handler is able to articulate the dog's alert.
- Must describe his search plan and be able to justify the plan, if necessary.
- Must be able to control the dog and conduct a thorough search.
- Must recognize the dog's alert and advise the evaluator when a source has been located.
- The team fails the test if the handler calls an alert on the animal remains.

Figure 3.1 Framework for basic cadaver K-9 team proficiency test

K-9 Specialty Search Associates **CADAVER DOG PROFICIENCY EVALUATION**		
Date:	Location:	
Handler:	Dog:	
Weather:	Wind.	Temperature:
Time set·	Time worked.	Time delay·
Scent source	Number of plants·	Number of neutral plants
Location (above/buried)	Depth	Type soil

In an area of approximately ________ the K-9 must locate and correctly identify a scent source(s). The handler must properly direct the search, taking into consideration the wind, weather, terrain and the type of search being conducted The test is conducted on a pass/fail basis.

RATINGS. O = OUTSTANDING | E = EXCELLENT | S = SATISFACTORY | NI = NEEDS IMPROVEMENT | F = FAILURE

K-9 OBEDIENT TO HANDLERS COMMAND	
EAGERNESS OF THE K-9 TO WORK	
HANDLER IS ABLE TO ARTICULATE THE K-9 ALERT	
K-9 RANGING DISTANCE (TO CONDITIONS)	
HANDLER ADJUSTS SEARCH PATTERNS FOR CHANGING CONDITIONS	
K-9 AVOIDS DISTRACTIONS	
HANDLER IS ALERT TO VISUAL CLUES	
DOG PERFORMS A READABLE ALERT	
HANDLER RECOGNITION OF K-9 ALERT	
HANDLER PROPERLY REWARDS DOG	

SCORE: **PASS** **FAIL**

COMMENTS

Start	________
Dog indicates:	________
Alert called	________

EVALUATOR SIGNATURE HANDLER SIGNATURE:

Figure 3.2 Sample of cadaver dog proficiency evaluation form

GENERAL GUIDELINES FOR TRAINING AND PRACTICE

There are a number of general guidelines that should be followed throughout training and in practice. These are summarized below:

- Consistently reward at (or as close to) the source as possible.
- Mark the desired behavior consistently. Timing is critical. Using a clicker can provide better timing. It buys additional time to reinforce the dog if you are not immediately able to do it, since the clicker means the reward is coming.
- Make sure the animal is performing consistently at the current level before proceeding to the next.
- Do not hesitate to work an easier, more basic exercise if the dog has problems at the current level.
- Assure that there are many repetitions of the exercise at each level.

TRAINING SUGGESTIONS

The following is a list of suggestions for training situations.

1. At the start of each training session, the team should work a simple problem in which the handler knows the location of the scent source. This can be a small area search, but it will allow the dog to be properly reinforced for the trained alert. This also motivates the dog and assures that it knows it is time to work.
2. Problems above ground may be set up in advance so that the scent cone is well distributed before the team begins the training session. This will give the handler experience observing the dog work a scent cone for a distance before reaching the source.
3. The training officer should consider the topography of the terrain, probable scent flow, weather, vegetation, and soil density when planning the training exercise. The time of day will affect the strength of available scent, since it will be weakest during the warmest period. If a team experiences a problem with detecting scent, have them work the same problem either in the early morning or late afternoon. After the air cools, there is a more available scent. Each factor has a definite impact upon the exercise and may contribute to the success or failure of the team.
4. Once the team has become proficient, the scent source can be weakened. This will require the handler to refine his or her search tactics in order to be successful.
5. If the team cannot successfully complete an exercise, the trainer should set up a simple, quick reinforcement exercise. Each team should finish the training session a winner.

6. The trainer should vary the scent material used. Pseudo Corpse™, soil samples, human blood, and human hair all can make good training aids. Blood can be fairly fresh or allowed to decompose before use. Human hair can be used as is or mixed with soil and water, aged, and then used.
7. The training exercises should be varied, including an occasional live victim. The source should be placed in a variety of configurations. Use brush piles, debris, leaves or heavy brush to conceal the training aid.

TRAINING SCENARIOS

It is beyond the scope of this book to cover more than just the basic training scenarios. However, some forensic situations require that systematic training has occurred and is documented: line-ups, vehicle searches, and distractors.

TRAINING FOR LINE-UPS

Line-ups are special search situations usually set up to test an array of articles or vehicles for the presence of decomposition scent. There are two reasons for training the cadaver dog for line-ups:

1. To identify residual decomposition scent on clothing items or in a vehicle (see also Chapter 11, Scent Line-ups);
2. To teach the dog to work a close, slow search.

Line-up searches performed for a court or judge should only be done by handler/canine teams that have been trained to do them.

Several exercises can be used to teach this skill. Start with a number of cloth items placed approximately six feet apart. For the first few repetitions, use sterile gauze pads in jelly jars with pierced tops. Five jars are placed in the line. One pad will have been scented with Pseudo Corpse™ Formulation II.

The dog is started with its search command at one end and worked, on leash, down the line. Initially the dog will probably work fast and overshoot the target. Do not correct, but when you reach the end of the line, turn around and start back, this time targeting the dog on each item. Watch for a change of body language when the dog reaches the target. As the dog investigates the target, cue it to perform the trained alert. As soon as the dog alerts, reward it close to the source.

Work the line several times, concentrating on slowing the dog and cueing the alert as soon as the dog shows scent recognition at the target. Make sure it is rewarded each time at the "hot" source. After 4–5 repetitions, change the position of the negative containers, so that the hot container does not remain in the same position. For example, if the initial position of the hot container is #3, change it to #4 from one end. Then work the dog from both ends; this way the hot container is fourth from one end and second from the other end.

After a number of repetitions, the animal should be performing its conditioned alert automatically when it reaches the target. The object is to have the dog react to the presence of the target odor. To check the animal's reliability, set up another line-up with all negative scent sources. Move the negative bottles used in the previous exercise to a new area. Give the dog its search command and work the line. There should be no reaction to any of the objects. Once you finish the line and the dog has not made any indication, reward it.

The second phase involves using items with other scents on them, as well as one with the cadaver-training scent. For this phase, collect T-shirts from several subjects. Place a scented gauze pad inside one of the shirts. Place them about six feet apart, four or five in a line, and work the same way as in the previous exercise.

Remember that you are presenting several scented items to the dog, so there may be some initial confusion. Treat it as a new exercise, drop your criteria, and cue the dog if necessary at the cadaver-scented item.

During the initial process, once the dog reliably performs the task on lead, try working the line-up off lead. Since the dog can read human body language well and handlers occasionally have a tendency to signal where the hot item is in the line-up by slowing or stopping, off lead work will allow the dog to make up its mind without a cue from the handler.

Initially give the dog its search command and stand at one end of the line. Allow the dog to proceed down the line alone. If the dog indicates on a negative item, give a verbal "wrong, get to work" or "leave it." Watch carefully for any indication when the dog reaches the hot item. Give the dog time to make a decision. If it performs the desired indication on its own, reward immediately! If the dog hesitates before alerting, cue it from a distance and immediately reward as soon as the alert is performed.

Once the animal reliably indicates the target scent on its own and performs its alert, you can proceed to work a line-up "blind." Have another person set up the problem. Make sure that person then watches the exercise so he or she can inform you if the dog indicates on a negative item, so your verbal correction can be immediate. When the dog is correct, make sure it is rewarded immediately.

Do the first few blind problems on lead. This places you close to the dog and allows more immediate correction or reward. Then try the blind line-up off lead. If you wish, walk down the line with the dog. Otherwise stand at one end and let the dog work independently. However, be sure you require your full trained alert from the dog.

TRAINING FOR VEHICLE SEARCHES

Since the dog has been familiarized with searching for and indicating residual cadaver scent, training for *vehicle search* is primarily concerned with introducing the animal to a new search situation with different ambient odors

Since dogs may become excited while searching vehicles, it is a good idea to locate a junkyard or use vehicles in an impound yard for initial training. Some vehicle owners will get upset if a dog jumps up on the car and scratches it. Check and make sure the vehicles used have not been involved in an accident with serious injuries or fatality, since residual (now decomposed) blood may interfere with training.

Start with more than one vehicle. For the first few repetitions, place the scent tube under the rear bumper. Most cars have bumper brackets that will hold the tube. The source should be on the second or third vehicle to be checked.

Initial searches should be done on lead. This enables the handler to control the dog's movement, focus it on the task at hand, and target areas of the vehicle if necessary.

Work with a loose lead and keep the dog between you and the vehicle if it does not initially focus. Target specific areas of the vehicles including the door and trunk seams. When the dog enters the zone where it first encounters the target odor, there should be a definite change it its body language and a change in its breathing pattern. The dog may try to access the source prior to performing the desired indication. From the onset, if the dog does not perform the desired alert immediately, cue and then reward. For a second repetition, start the search at another vehicle so the dog does not automatically expect to find the source on, say, the third vehicle.

Then change the vehicle sequence and also the type of vehicle used as the target. When the dog is accustomed to searching cars, vary the placement of the scent source to include the interior and the trunk. When first placing the scent in the trunk, leave it cracked open so there is adequate scent flow for the dog to detect easily. Then place a source in the closed trunk and leave it for several hours, then work the car. The dog should be able to detect the odor and alert without the trunk being opened.

Vary the scent sources. Use decomposing blood, cloths containing Pseudo Scent™, or even soil samples. Work on problems until the dog alerts reliably. Once you are satisfied with the progress, do a blind search. The dog must perform its trained alert as soon as it locates the source. Be sure the person placing the scent is there to guide you in rewarding the dog correctly.

TRAINING FOR DISTRACTORS

It is important that the dog indicate only human remains in an area. Since it is not possible to control what might be in a search area, non-human animal remains—*distractors*— should be introduced during the training process. We do not allow the dog to alert on non-human remains.

Procedure

- For training purposes collect road kill.
- Place the road kill in the training area. It should be placed so that the dog encounters the animal before reaching the area where a human source is located.
- Place the human decomposition scent source.
- Give the dog its search cue and proceed to search the area.
- If the dog passes by the animal without acknowledging it, let it continue the search.
- If the dog goes to the animal and investigates it, tell the dog to "leave it, get to work" and continue the search.
- If the dog begins to give its trained indication on the animal, give it a sharp "no" and continue the search.
- Effusively reward the dog when it locates and alerts on the source.

Most dogs will show some interest in the animal. The majority will just check it and continue on. They seem to be able to differentiate between animal and human when properly imprinted.

When the handler is confident that the dog will not alert on the non-human remains, bury them in the same area where you have a positive buried source. Follow the above steps doing a search for a buried source.

ONGOING TRAINING REGIME

Once training is complete and the team has been tested, it is essential to practice on at least a weekly basis. The practice sessions should be a combination of situations that allow the team to test basic skills and as well as new challenges. The best practice regime includes occasional but regular work with a trainer. This prevents bad habits from creeping into either dog or handler behavior.

It is highly recommended that the handler keep accurate and ongoing training records, noting each training session date and basic activities. This is a valuable documentation of the quality of the dog. It also gives the handler data in developing training regimes, problem solving, and skill improvement.

FREQUENTLY ASKED QUESTIONS

What breed of dog is best?

Many different of dog breeds are appropriate. Generally the breeds classified as "working" dogs work best. Most common are the German Shepherd, the Labrador and Golden Retrievers, and some of the "herding breeds." Just as important as breed is the intelligence and personality of the dog and its desire to please the handler. A dog with high "prey" drive, one that enjoys interactive "ball" play, will adapt better to cadaver dog work.

How old should the dog be before training begins?

It is possible to begin training at any age. If you are starting a puppy, you can play "scent" games with it beginning at 10–12 weeks of age. Remember that a puppy has a limited attention span so you should not proceed too rapidly. Also a young dog (normally under one year of age) has not reached its full growth. So, even if the dog works well in training, it may not have developed the physical and mental stamina to work an actual search. The dog also needs to be well socialized and have a good foundation of basic obedience training.

Where can I find a good trainer?

There are several qualities that you should look for in a trainer. Determine whether he or she

- Has experience in training specialty scent search dogs.
- Conducts a logical and systematic training program.
- Uses the principles of positive reinforcement.
- Has a proven track record both with his or her own dog(s) and with students that have completed the program..

You may want to work with a trainer who has worked in the law enforcement field, training drug or other specialty search dogs. Any program you select should be broken down into small, logical steps. The trainer should ensure that the student is fluent in one step before moving on to the next. Scent training must be done using positive reinforcement. It is very difficult to get a dog to search enthusiastically using force methods. Trainers should be able to demonstrate both the individual steps and the finished product with their own animals.

Where can I get training materials?

See Chapter 4 and Appendix A for a discussion of how to make or obtain training materials.

My dog is trained for search and rescue. Can I also train it for cadaver work?

Most dogs are very capable of multi-tasking. First analyze what your major use will be. If it is wilderness area search or trailing, train that as the primary task. Once the dog is well into the program, then you may begin to train cadaver search as the secondary task. It is better to separate the training sessions so the dog is only concentrating on one skill at a time. Once the dog is reliable you may occasionally combine the two tasks in one session, i.e., an air scent problem with both a live and deceased subject.

I've started training my dog using the blocks, but it gets bored. Shouldn't I just start doing larger areas instead of the mechanical imprinting.

No. There are two reasons for working mechanical imprinting. First, it provides controlled introduction to the desired odor(s) in a systematic manner that allows the handler to teach the desired indication through multiple repetitions. Secondly, it teaches the dog to search in a thorough manner under handler control.

If you proceed too rapidly, it will be more difficult to teach your desired alert and to teach the animal to search thoroughly. Remember that the handler controls both the training situation and a search, not the dog. Law enforcement dogs used for specialty scent work (narcotics, etc.) go through an intensive period of scent introduction and imprinting before they begin to work even small search problems.

Will the dog alert to dead animals?

Your dog can be proofed from alerting on animal remains if you introduce some during your training program. Place a road kill in your search area. The dog will probably be attracted to it. Watch the dog when it checks it out. If it gives the distractor a cursory sniff and then continues the search pattern, do nothing. If the dog pays a lot of attention to the animal, give it a strong "leave it" and praise when it does. If the dog should give an alert, the admonition "No, get back to work" should work.

During a search, if you see your dog nosing around in an area and suspect it is animal, check it. You want to make sure the item is animal and not from a disarticulated human body.

How long does it take to have an adequately trained dog?

Several factors come into play: the amount of time you spend training and the native ability of the dog to adapt to search work are a couple of them. Each dog progresses at its own speed. We have had handlers leave a seven-day class and immediately have a find. However that does not mean that they have a completely trained cadaver dog.

Training is ongoing. You need to work the dog in as many scenarios, terrain and conditions as possible. The team should be periodically evaluated to assess their proficiency. We normally work with our own new dogs for approximately one year before we will work them as the primary dogs during a search. Otherwise we will work an experienced dog through its search area as confirmation of a negative area.

My dog located a body during the search and was hesitant to approach. Why?

During training we work with small scent sources in a container. When the dog locates a real body, there is much more scent available. This larger scent source may actually be overwhelming to the animal, especially if the body is in a putrefied state. The dog also may not have made the connection between the odor and the visual impact of a human. When humans had contact with the dog prior to this, they have normally been alive and responsive to the animal. Thus, the dog initially may hesitate, hackle, cower, or even back off completely. It may also try to elicit a response from the subject, or mark it by urinating or defecating on or near it.

We use a full size mannequin during training to simulate both aboveground remains and a hanging victim. It is liberally scented, clothed, and placed in a realistic position. This allows the dog to find a larger scent source with the visual impact of finding a person.

Another way to overcome the hesitation is to introduce the dog to a body on a real search. Once the subject is located, and with the approval of the responsible agency, you may be able to walk your dog up to the subject. Use quiet verbal praise while you approach and reinforce the dog liberally after the introduction. Do not let your dog urinate, defecate or touch the body! It is not a good idea to use this approach if family members are in the area.

Will my dog become depressed after finding a body?

Dogs are trained to find scent. They do not associate the scent with something unpleasant. A dog does not experience the same emotions as its human partner. However, the dog can read the handler's emotions very well; if the handler becomes depressed or upset, the dog may become subdued.

Environmental stress during the search can have a significant impact on the dog. This is especially evident during extended searches where the dog works for long periods or at a disaster situation where the handler and dog are working under extremely stressful conditions. In most situations, however, the animal simply makes the find and wants its reward.

I always set out three scent sources when I plan a training session. Now my dog will find one, then continue to search the area until it locates the other two. Then it will alert and proceed to show me where all three sources are located. How can I correct it so the dog will alert on each one as it finds them?

A dog can become conditioned to multiple finds. If the handler observes the dog doing its original alert (body language, not the trained indication) on a source, and then allows the dog to leave it and continue to locate the others before it performs its trained indication on one, then it is time to vary the training program.

Go back and put only one source in the area. When the dog goes to the source and leaves it, call it back and have it indicate, rewarding it for the find. Then have it continue to search the area and acknowledge the negative search. In the future, you can set up the training problem with more than one source, but make sure the dog indicates the source and is rewarded before being instructed to "search for more."

I was doing a search for disarticulated bones and my dog alerted in some vegetation. When I looked there wasn't any visible indication of remains and we couldn't find any when we searched the area. Why?

More than likely some flesh or decomposition fluid dropped to the ground while being carried by an animal. The odor will remain in the earth or on the leaves and the dog will indicate.

When starting your search for disarticulated, scattered remains, watch the dog closely when it does its free search to acclimate to the area. Its actions may give you an idea of the scatter pattern, since fluid may have been deposited on the ground or vegetation as scavengers dragged or carried a portion of the body from the original site.

How long should I work my dog during a search?

Cadaver search, especially for buried remains, is intense nasal activity. We generally work our dogs for 20 minutes then water and rest them for 10 minutes. Of course, your working time is also governed by environmental conditions. In extreme heat, the best time to search with maximum effectiveness is generally the early morning hours, rather than during the heat of the day.

In all search situations, make sure the dog is offered water frequently. Water assists in keeping the nasal passages moistened and working more effectively.

Generally there is no necessity to do a cadaver search at night. The exception would be a missing person where there is an expectation that they may have survived.

If you are working an extended search, have a reinforcement area set up so the dog can work and make a find. Being rewarded does wonders for the dog and reinforces the handler.

FINAL NOTE AND CAUTION

Cadaver dogs are a search tool and subject to an untold number of variables working a search. There may be a situation where the dog fails to locate a subject for a variety of reasons. When you inform the agency that an area is "clear" or make the determination to "dig here," not only is your reputation on the line, but so is the agency's perception of all search dogs.

Train your dog to be the most effective resource within your ability. Conduct your search in a logical and systematic manner. Do not be afraid to admit to an agency that a certain search is beyond your capability. Report your search responsibly. Do not be afraid to suggest that the agency use other resources to confirm your dog's work.

CHAPTER 4

TRAINING MATERIALS

CREATING AND HANDLING TRAINING AIDS

There a number of scent sources that are used in effective cadaver dog training. These include several natural scent sources and several artificial scent sources. Each type of source requires that certain precautions be observed to protect both the handler and the dog from possible injury or disease.

As training progresses, a number of different types of training aids will be acquired. With some common sense rules, the handler will be able to obtain, handle, and store all types with a minimum of risk.

SCENT SOURCES

Natural Scent: Human Flesh

Human flesh is the most authentic scent source. Flesh can be decomposed to any stage of putrefaction that the trainer desires. It requires refrigeration once the desired stage is reached to prevent further decay.

Obtaining human flesh is difficult. Certain states have legislation prohibiting its use for canine training. It may be obtained from a medical examiner or a coroner under certain controlled situations.

Decomposition creates corrosive by-products that can eat through metal containers. All decomposing flesh should be kept in glass or plastic. The trainer should wear gloves when handling any of these materials. Flesh may be a carrier of infectious bacteria or viral disease. When it is placed outside for training, the scent may attract carrion feeders.

Natural Scent: Human Blood

Human blood is authentic and can be aged to different stages of putrefaction. Refrigeration is required to prevent decay. Blood is a good scent source for simulating crime scenes, and for residual scent work. It also can be buried in soil to mimic a buried body.

Blood can be obtained from a willing donor or a medical facility. It may sometimes be possible to obtain outdated blood from a blood bank or the Red Cross. If it is obtained from a medical source, blood may have anticoagulants or other chemical additives. Shipping containers are subject to the same policy for disposal as any other medical waste.

Bandaging materials soaked with blood may also be used. These can be obtained from medical sources.

The handler must wear protective gloves at all times when setting up problems. Avoid splatters. Blood may transmit disease, so cleaning up residual amounts is extremely important.

Natural Scent: Soil Samples

Soil dug from a body site provides an authentic source. This dirt contains a wide range of the by-products of decomposition and putrefaction. It is relatively easy to handle and can be used to simulate a wide variety of training scenarios.

The sample can be dug from any site where a body has decomposed. It can be maintained in plastic bags and does not require refrigeration, unless it is not going to be used for a long period of time. If samples are acquired from different types of soil, they will vary in odor strength. The variation of odor will help in training for older burials.

It will be necessary to obtain legitimate access to burial sites to acquire the samples. Make sure that they are dug from the proper area. It also helps to dig some negative samples from the surrounding area to provide a basis for assessing the dog's alert.

Use care in handling by wearing gloves to prevent contact. Since the odor of some samples may be strong, transport in plastic bags inside an airtight container, such as an ammunition can. Be sure to keep these corrosive materials in plastic rather than metal containers.

If the sample becomes extremely dry and the scent becomes weak, add a few drops of water. The additional moisture will allow bacterial action to resume.

Natural Scent: Adipocere

Adipocere is a by-product of decomposition in a wet or damp environment and is an authentic source. It makes an excellent training aid, but requires access to a body site to obtain. Store it in a glass or plastic container. Wear gloves when handling. The material does not require refrigeration unless it is not to be used for a long time.

Artificial Scent: Putrescine (1,4 – Diaminobutane) and Cadaverine (1,5 – Diaminopentane)

Putrescine and *cadaverine* are chemicals that provide a convenient vehicle for the imprinting and reinforcement of dogs for cadaver search. They are all di-amino compounds, similar to those created during the process of decomposition of organic matter that remain in the environment for a substantial period of time. It only requires a small amount of these chemicals (1-5 drops) for a valid scent source.

These compounds are toxic and pose a possible health hazard to both the handler and the dog. Both compounds crystallize if the ambient temperature is too low and may need to be warmed in a water bath to be usable.

The following safety precautions should be followed:

- Prevent inhalation of fumes by opening the container in a well ventilated area.
- Prevent absorption through the skin by wearing protective gloves while handling.

Since the compounds are corrosive, transport the chemicals in a protective container to prevent the accidental breakage of the bottle. Use a bottle with a Teflon™ cap for storage. The liquid will eat through the rubber bulb of an eyedropper, if the dropper is used as a bottle cap.

Artificial scent: Sigma Pseudo™ Corpse I (for early detection) Sigma Pseudo™ Corpse II (for post-putrefaction detection) Sigma Pseudo™ Distressed Body (detection of nonresponsive live victims)

These chemicals replicate different stages of decomposition. They are easy to handle since they are packaged in single-dose vials. They do not require any special care in storage and are safe for the environment.

Set-up should be done in a well ventilated area. Since the chemicals are packaged in 1-ml vials, more than one may be needed for some training problems.

SCENTED TRAINING AIDS

The artificial or natural scent sources can be placed on toys (tennis balls or Kongs™), in tubes (scent tubes), or in jar containers (scent jars). The scent source is first placed on a gauze pad, then put into the container to prevent the dog from coming into contact with it. If artificial chemical scents are used, the vial is placed in the container. Instructions on preparing scented balls are given below.

To simulate a buried body, the scent source can also be placed directly in the soil after a hole has been dug. Cover it just as if burying a container. However, the aid will not be recoverable. If the same area is used frequently for training, the dog will alert on the same source for some time.

STORAGE CONTAINERS

Training aids may be kept in glass, plastic, and metal containers (for the outer container). Jelly jars with perforated and solid covers are useful for several purposes. Metal coffee cans, washed to remove oils, with a tight fitting plastic lid are readily available and convenient. Use a freezer-weight resealable plastic bag for soil samples and adipocere to prevent corrosion. There are metal evidence cans available as well.

For pungent samples, the military style ammunition cans are ideal. They seal tightly and can hold several individual containers.

TRAINING CONTAINERS

Several types of containers are suitable for the training aids. Coffee cans can be used. Puncture the plastic lid to prevent the dog from coming in contact with the material. After use, place a solid lid on the can.

Glass and plastic containers can also be used. Jelly jar tops can be perforated to allow scent flow, or a lid can be fashioned from screen material, held on with a plumbing clamp.

See Chapter 12 for a discussion of scent pumps and scent cans used for water search training.

Scent Tube

Materials needed for one scent tube—one each:

- 1-1/2 inch ABS pipe about 6 inches in length
- 1-1/2 inch female adapter
- 1-1/2 inch threaded plug
- Cap for 1-1/2 inch pipe

The most practical for many applications is the "scent tube." These protect the scent source for the dog and allow it to be handled safely. It is fashioned from ABS pipe. The black plastic is preferred because it is not easily seen by the handler, which helps prevent cueing the dog as to the article's location. Make enough of them so that there are some "negatives." The negative tubes can be placed in the training area to prevent the dog from orienting to the object (the tube itself) rather than the scent.

Cut a piece of pipe about 6 inches long. Drill a number of 1/4-inch holes in the pipe to allow the scent to flow freely. Install the cap on one end and the female adapter on the other. Thread the plug into the female adapter. The plug makes it easy to change scent sources in the tube. Since the caps fit tightly, it is not necessary to use pipe cement. If the trainer desires, eyebolts can be installed in the caps for hanging the container. The scent tube can be buried, hung, used in the water, or used as a throw toy to improve scent commitment in a weak dog. Use nylon knee-high hose to contain soil within the scent tube.

See Chapter 12 and Appendix A for information about scent cages and scent pumps (see also Figure 4.1).

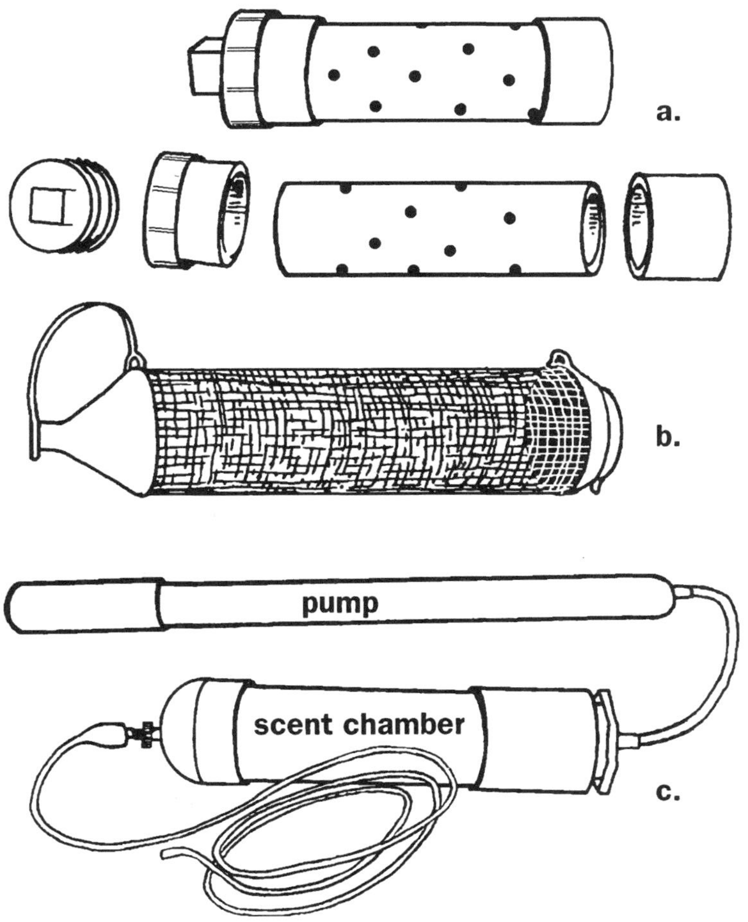

Figure 4.1 a) Scent tube; b) Scent cage; c) Scent pump

Scented Toys

A gauze pad can be scented with Sigma Pseudo™ Corpse and placed inside a Kong™. Tennis balls may be scented with the chemical. Place a chemically scented gauze pad in a small container such as a jelly jar with a perforated top, and put into a clean, larger container such as a washed coffee can. Place balls in the larger container, seal and leave for 24 hours. The tennis ball will retain the odor; however, it will not have caustic chemical residue on the surface. Nevertheless, handle the ball with disposable gloves to avoid scent transfer. Once the dog is giving good scent recognition the scented ball can be placed on the ground among several unscented ones and the dog can be asked to indicate it.

If you use due care, the various types of training aids may be used over and over.

EQUIPMENT AND SET-UP NEEDED FOR IMPRINTING PHASE

- 6 to 12 concrete blocks
- Sterile gauze pads
- Jelly jars with perforated and solid covers
- Disposable gloves
- Scent material (Sigma Pseudo™ Corpse Formulation I & II)
- Reward (food or toy), and a clicker if you use one for training

Formulation II is generally used for the first scent recognition activities. It seems to present a stronger scent picture, and the dogs react faster. Formulation I is introduced when the trainer begins to vary the scent sources.

Set up the training context as follows:

1. Place the contents of one vial of Formulation II on a sterile gauze pad.
2. Place the gauze pad in a jelly jar with a perforated top.
3. Place 5 concrete blocks in a *scent line* and put the jar in the 4th or 5th block.
4. Put the chemical on the gauze at least 1/2 hour prior to starting your training. This allows the gauze to dry. If desired, negative jars can be placed in the remaining blocks. Following the training session, seal the jar containing the scent source with a solid top. The source will remain viable for several sessions.

EQUIPMENT NEEDED AS TRAINING PROGRESSES

- Scent tubes
- Nylon knee-high hose
- Soil
- Dried blood
- Decomposition fluid
- Flesh
- Human bone
- Additional scent sources (if available and desired)

CHAPTER 5

PROFESSIONAL ISSUES

STANDARDIZATION AND CERTIFICATION

There is currently no set of standards and no national certification specifically for cadaver dogs. Several trainers offer proficiency tests, such as the one described in Chapter 3. These proficiency tests offer limited certification. Dog handlers can also become qualified as expert witnesses within a given jurisdiction as a result of their involvement with court testimony.

ETHICS AND PROFESSIONAL CONDUCT

It is essential that you conduct your training, searching, and involvement with the court with the highest professional standards of honesty, discretion, and respect for colleagues and for the court system. Conclusions from a search should be based on evidence, not speculation.

LEVELS OF CERTAINTY AND CONCLUSIONS REACHED

Individuals requesting a search are understandably going to want to know the level of certainty with which the search was carried out. Obviously if the victim is found, the level of certainty is 100 percent. The real issue occurs when nothing is found and the person requesting the search wants to know whether to cross an area off of his or her list. This is particularly true when the police have requested a search based on information obtained during the course of an investigation.

No one can ever be 100 percent certain that a negative search means the deceased is not in the search area. Multiple variables exist, including but certainly not limited to the handler, the dog, the terrain, the weather, the time since presumed death, and the physical features of the missing person.

Handler/dog teams differ. A handler may misread a dog or fail to see a partial alert or area of interest because of ground cover or foliage. A dog may not be working well. This is often obvious to the handler, but at other times it may be missed. A physical ailment may cause a dog to skip an area because of the terrain. A dog that has traveled a long distance may fail to acclimate and will not search well.

The effects of terrain on search outcome are discussed in detail in other chapters. It is always important to remember that soil type will affect the search. Sandy soil is more likely to permit scent escape than is clay. Dry soil will permit scent escape more than wet soil. Steep terrain will interfere with search patterns and may provide areas seemingly inaccessible. Heavy growth, particularly brambles, may prevent a dog from searching an area. These types of secondary growth can occur over a very short time and may well not have been present when and if a body was buried on the site.

Weather is also discussed in detail in other chapters. Suffice it to say that temperature, humidity, wind direction and speed, and barometric pressure can all affect the outcome of a search. Heat is particularly debilitating to dogs and may further affect the search by promoting exhaustion and dehydration.

Bodies have been recovered more than 30 years after burial. Admittedly, this is exceptional, but must be remembered when evaluating the probability of a successful search. Decomposition rates vary with depths of burial, soil type, and amount of moisture. Climate can play an important role as well, particularly in the more northern latitudes subject to frost. Weather obviously plays a bigger role when one is searching for an individual missing and presumed dead, but not thought to be buried.

The physical characteristics of the missing individual include sex, height, weight, and degree of conditioning. A large, obese person is going to provide a greater scent pool. Infants, on the other hand, have little tissue and the scent source will be lost much sooner.

It is also relevant to know what the individual was supposedly wearing. A full set of clothing may retard decomposition. Sometimes an unburied individual who has been wrapped up in material such as a blanket will be better preserved than one buried without such covering. Unfortunately, the covering itself may serve to retard scent escape.

Depending on the area of the country, the role of *carnivores, omnivores,* and other *taphonomic agents* (see Chapter 9) must be considered. Bodies in the Northeast, for example, are subject to predation and scatter by bear, coyote, and domestic dog. Rodents and corvids (crows and ravens) may also contribute to the scattering of human remains, particularly small bones and teeth.

The handler is responsible for reporting the search and its results. Weighing all the variables, a negative search may be reported to a general, *but never absolute,* degree of certainty. If the level of certainty falls below 50 percent, it is probably worthwhile to search the area with a different team or on a different day. If new information heightens the likelihood that the missing person is in the area searched, then re-searching should be carried out regardless of the believed degree of certainty.

RECORD KEEPING

Good records are a necessity for the working dog handler. They provide valid documentation of your training, actual search work, and experience of both the dog and the handler.

There are three types of records that you should maintain. They are (1) a training log; (2) search reports; and (3) handler resume. Each record covers a different facet of your activities and, taken as a whole, presents a history of your experience.

TRAINING RECORDS

The *training log* provides a chronological history of all training activities of the K-9 team (see Appendix B for examples). This record starts with the initial puppy scent work. It records frequency of training, progress made, weaknesses noted, and corrective actions taken. The individual record exists in addition to any unit records of training sessions.

The log allows you to review your work and can be used by a trainer or evaluator to judge the level of performance of the team. These records, since they are kept "in the normal course of business," are admissible in court should you be called to testify in a criminal or civil case. Training records provide a portion of the documentation necessary to qualify you to testify in a court case.

Training records can be kept on a form in a loose-leaf notebook, as a journal, on computer, or simply as entries in a pocket notebook. The format is not as important as insuring that all the pertinent information is recorded. We recommend a prepared form kept in a loose-leaf binder. Using a form ensures no information is omitted inadvertently.

The training record form should includethe following items:

1. Dog's name
2. Handler's name
3. Training location
4. Type of terrain
5. Type of search
6. Type of training aid

7. Time problem set: time worked: time delay
8. How much time involved in search
9. Weather conditions: temperature; wind speed and direction; precipitation (if any)
10. If a buried problem, type of soil and depth of burial
11. Narrative description of search
12. Whether the dog located the source and type of alert
13. If training problem was set up by someone other than the handler, record name
14. Date of training
15. Signature or trainer's signature

Keep records up to date. Enter the information accurately and honestly. You are your own best critic. Document both the good and bad sessions. If you note a weak area, record the training exercises you perform to overcome the problem.

SEARCH REPORTS

Each actual case that you work should be documented in a *search report* describing your activity from the time you are called out until the final debriefing (see Appendix B for examples). Even if you did not make the actual find, the record of your activity provides information about the overall conduct of the search, including time spent and area covered, as well as both positive and negative results. This is extremely important during an on-going operation or if the search is suspended, then reactivated. Many searches initiate or extend forensic investigations; thus, documents about them eventually may be used in court.

Much of the information needed for a good search report is similar to the training record. The report should be completed as soon as practical after the completion of the search.

Information necessary for the report includes the following items:

1. Handler and canine credentials
2. Who requested the search, agency requesting, date, and stated purpose
3. Information about the case, including victim identity and unique characteristics, potential cause and manner of death, date last seen, details known about the search location
4. Structural details about the search, including date, location, personnel present, times of dispatch, arrival, search commencement, and search completion
5. Technical details about the search, including precipitation, temperature, wind speed and direction, terrain and ground cover, potential barriers to air flow, potential areas of false alert, and potential areas of danger to the dog or handler

6. Search strategy and implementation, dog behavior (expressed interest, alerts, problems), interpretation of behavior, alterations of search strategy, results of search, and evaluation of strengths and weaknesses of the search effort
7. Discovery and recovery of remains, if appropriate, including chain of custody
8. Map of area searched and location of remains found
9. Signature and date of report completion

The narrative should contain information regarding your activities in your search area. If you are unable to delineate your search area by easily described landmarks, indicate the area on a map. If you search more than one area, make sure all search areas are listed. If there is a question at a later date regarding a specific area, all areas covered in the overall search will be listed. The collective reports of the individual search teams will document the scope of the entire search.

You should attach any maps or sketches you make to your original. You can also attach copies of news clippings about the search to your copy. The original should be maintained by the handler, and copies of the reports from all the teams involved should become part of the unit records. Completed reports may be kept in a section of a binder or file.

RESUME

The *resume* is a summary of your personal experience and a history of your involvement in cadaver searches, other forms of *air scent search*, and/or *search and rescue*. Each handler should maintain a record of his or her training and experience and that of the dog (see Appendix B for examples).

The resume should contain the following information:

1. Summary of your involvement in the field
2. All training received
3. All specialty training you have attended
4. Any special recognition you have been accorded
5. Number of dogs you have trained

You should also compile a short resume for your dog, which should includethe following items:

1. Registered and call name
2. Breed and date of birth
3. When you acquired the dog
4. When you started training
5. When the dog was certified for use
6. A brief summary (date and location) of the dog's search work

This compilation is extremely important if you should be required to testify in court. A complete record of your training and experience adds credibility to your testimony. Once you have developed your resume, make sure you keep it updated with any additional training or activities that are pertinent. Remember, the purpose of good records is not to maintain a "brag book." Good, up-to-date records of your work provide credibility and, if needed for court, portray you and your dog as professionals in search work.

EVALUATING THE QUALIFICATIONS OF AN UNKNOWN DOG/HANDLER TEAM

If you have not worked with the team previously, there are a number of criteria that you can use to evaluate their qualifications.

1. Training qualifications—type received
2. Recommendations of another law enforcement agency
3. Record of searches the team has worked and results
4. Informal testing of the team. Each handler possesses training materials for reinforcement. The material can be hidden in a predetermined area by an officer, as a blind test for the team.

TESTIFYING IN COURT

Every K-9 handler, police officer, or volunteer may receive a *subpoena* to testify in court regarding his or her activities and observations during a search. Your testimony may be necessary to detail the discovery of a crime scene.

There is no need to be nervous about your testimony if you have properly documented your training and filed a report of the search. The training log establishes a foundation for credibility for you as a handler and the overall performance of your dog under a variety of circumstances. The search report documents your activities and findings during a specific search.

There are certain steps you should take when you receive a subpoena.

1. Update your resume.
2. Prepare a resume for your dog, including all training and cases worked.
3. Schedule a meeting with the District Attorney who is the case prosecutor. If possible, meet in advance of your court date. He or she will brief you on exactly what testimony is needed. If possible, generally outline the questions he will ask you. This is the time to discuss all the details of the case. You want to be prepared before you take the stand. Neither you nor

the District Attorney want any surprise questions or answers when you are on the witness stand, under oath.

4. Bring copies of your resume, the dog's resume, and your report with you to the meeting so they can be reviewed.
5. On the date you are scheduled to testify, make sure you arrive in court before your appointed time.
6. Dress appropriately. Some jurisdictions will allow uniforms, however, most require that witnesses, including police officers, wear civilian clothing. Make sure you present a neat, professional appearance.
7. Be prepared to be sequestered. Most defense attorneys request that the witness be kept out of the courtroom prior to testifying. Therefore, you will not be able to hear other witnesses' versions of events.
8. Present a professional image on the witness stand. Relax but be businesslike. Speak clearly. Pay attention to the attorney questioning you; however, direct your answers to the jury.
9. Make sure to look at the jury as you talk. One favorite ploy of defense attorneys is to ask a question from the other side of the room.
10. Answer only the question that was asked. Keep your answer as brief as possible. Don't embellish your testimony. Elaborate on an answer only if requested.
11. Take your time before you answer. If you don't understand the question, ask to have it repeated.
12. If you need to refresh your memory, ask to refer to your report before answering. Remember, if your report has been submitted to the investigating agency and is part of the case file, the defense attorney has a copy obtained under the rules of disclosure.

A trial is an adversarial procedure. The defense attorney is going to attempt to discredit your testimony. One of the favorite questions is "Have you discussed this case with anyone prior to your court appearance?" If you answer "No," he or she probably has you in a box. Of course you have talked to someone about the case, even if only to discuss your testimony with the prosecutor in your pre-trial meeting. This discrepancy is enough to allow the defense to attempt to question your credibility.

Do not let the defense attorney harass you. He or she may belabor some minor point, but do not lose your cool. If he or she begins to badger you, it is the job of the prosecutor to object and get the questioning back on track.

If you keep these few pointers in mind, you will make an extremely favorable impression on the jury. Your testimony will have to be presented in a professional manner. Juries love to hear dog testimony, so you will be well received. As long as you relate your evidence in a credible manner, you have provided assistance in the presentation of the prosecution's case.

QUALIFYING THE DOG/HANDLER TEAM AS AN EXPERT WITNESS

Before you testify, the prosecutor will generally *qualify the witness* (including both the dog and handler) regarding their training and experience. Typical questions asked of a dog handler follow. Please note, the list is not exhaustive and is offered only as a guide..

Suggested questions to be asked of a dog handler:

1. State your name.
2. State your occupation. (K-9 handler for [volunteer group, police department])
3. How long have you been a dog handler?
4. What type of search do you perform with the dog?
5. With what breed of dog do you work?
6. What is the dog's name? Age?
7. Is this the first dog you have trained for search work?
8. When did you start training?
9. What requirements do and the dog have to meet before you are operational?
10. Did you graduate from a school or a course with your dog?
11. How long was the schooling?
12. Have you attended any other schools or seminars regarding dogs? When and where?
13. Do you and your dog participate in regular training sessions?
14. How often?
15. What is the purpose of these training sessions?
16. What do you use to train the dog to detect a body? (Pseudo Corpse™, soil samples)
17. Describe for the court your training procedure.
18. Describe for the court how your dog indicates it has made a "find."
19. What records are kept on the dog's training status?
20. Have you and your dog participated in actual searches for (live, cadaver, drowning)?
21. What records are kept on the dog's actual searches?
22. Directing your attention to (date), did you conduct a search with the dog? Where?
23. What was the nature of the case?
24. Who requested your presence?

25. How were you and your dog used in this case?
26. At what time did you arrive at the scene?
27. Please state what you observed at the scene.
28. What time did you start your search?
29. When you worked with your dog in this case, what were the weather conditions?
30. Describe for the court how you and your dog conducted the search.
31. How could you tell when your dog located (victim, scent)?
32. What did you do when your dog indicated it had located (victim, article, grave)?
33. Who did you notify?
34. Please describe what you observed.
35. When did you leave the scene?

CHAPTER 6

LEGAL ISSUES

INTRODUCTION

While there are a wide variety of legal issues dealing with animals, handlers need to be aware of the impact of the law in three particular areas. First, there is a need to be aware of issues surrounding licensure and vaccination. Second, handlers need to be aware of their possible liability for negligence. Finally, and perhaps most importantly, handlers need to have at least a passing knowledge of issues surrounding the Fourth Amendment and search and seizure.

LICENSURE AND VACCINATION

States may regulate and control animals under their police power. This power is exerted over dogs to a greater extent than perhaps any other domestic animal. The reason for this control lies principally in the need to prevent diseases such as rabies, and the recognized fact that dogs can and do cause damage to persons and property. This power of the state is often delegated to the cities and towns.

The statutes and ordinances regulating dogs must be reasonable. The licensing fee must bear a relationship to the acts proscribed. Among the statutory commandments are laws that prohibit dogs running free when not under the control of their owner/handler, authorize the wearing of a tag, punish excessive barking, and mandate certain vaccinations, particularly rabies.

Dogs used by search and rescue organizations or by various law enforcement agencies are not exempt from these laws. Additionally, having a license may aid in transporting a dog across state lines. Most states have some form of quarantine law. This law provides the state with a means of preventing disease by excluding animals either for a period of time or completely. The presence of a valid license gives state officials reasonable assurance that an animal is not harboring a communicable disease. Of course, federal laws and regulations can supersede state requirements in emergent or catastrophic situations.

EXERCISING "DUE CARE"

The second general area of law that handlers need to be aware of is *tort* law. Admittedly, legal scholars have difficulty adequately defining tort. For the purposes of this book, it will suffice to say that a tort is a wrongful act or omission. The act of omission can affect a legally protected interest in a person, property, or both. Two areas of law may be encountered when handling dogs. The first is *negligence* and the second is *strict liability*.

NEGLIGENCE

To prove negligence, a person must show that there was an act or omission by the handler, that the handler had a duty to exercise due care, that the handler breached his or her duty, that there is a causal relationship between the handler's conduct and the harm, and that damages resulted.

STRICT LIABILITY

Strict liability is "liability without fault." In certain circumstances, the law has developed a policy which states that a person has the right to recover damages despite the absence of fault on the part of the defendant. In other words, even if damage occurs through no fault of the defendant, the plaintiff may have the right to sue for damages. So strict liability is not absolute liability. Additionally, there are some defenses to strict liability.

The issues dealing with dogs are generally handled under strict liability. Some states also have specific statutes to deal with issues raised by inappropriate canine behavior. A handler may be found liable if his or her canine strays onto land not part of the search and causes damage. While there is an exception for domestic pets, this may not apply to the working canine.

Strict liability will also apply if the canine is known to be dangerous. The victim must show that the dog was in fact dangerous or vicious. Such evidence may include knowledge of a previous attack or bite, the behavior of the dog during the attack, etc. Size or breed cannot be used to demonstrate a dangerous propensity. However, it is important to realize that under strict liability, viciousness does not have to be proven. A handler will be found responsible even if the dog is one that barely has a mischievous desire to jump and nip. While the "one bite" rule is often mentioned, it has largely been replaced by statute. And most statutes do not in fact forgive that first bite.

JOINT AND SEVERAL LIABILITY

Tort law may impose *joint and several liability*. If the handler is not the owner of the dog, both may be liable. Similarly, an organized search and rescue group may be held liable for the act of one of its members. A department or municipality may be held liable for the act of one of its police officers.

SEARCH, SEIZURE, AND WARRANTS

When conducting a search, a dog/handler team is, in effect, searching for evidence. Most of the legal cases regarding dog searches deal with drug seizures, but the principle under which the issues are raised apply equally to cadaver dog searches. The two primary areas of concern are the acquisition of evidence and the acceptance of that evidence by a court. Unless the search team is operating within the guidelines set down by the Constitution of the United States and the court system, any evidence located during the search may not be admissible at a trial.

Searches made by cadaver dogs are covered by the laws of search and seizure in the U.S. Constitution. The Fourth Amendment provides that people shall be secure in their persons, houses, and possessions from unreasonable *search and seizure* and that no warrant to search shall be issued without *probable cause*. Any time a search is undertaken, issues regarding the necessity of a warrant arise. There are two areas which need to be understood when using dogs to carry out a search.

The first is whether a sniff constitutes a search. This particular question has limited applicability as regards cadaver dog searches. The legal focus is primarily on the activities of drug sniffing dogs. Initially, courts were divided on whether the use of a canine nose constituted a search (and thus was subject to the fourth amendment warrant provisions). Some courts concluded that the use of the canine nose was really no different than that of the officer's sense of smell. Other courts asserted that the dog was a "sense enhancing" police tool, no different than a flashlight or camera.

The matter finally reached the U.S. Supreme Court in the case of United States *v.* Place. The court decided that the activity of a drug sniffing dog was unique. The dog only alerted if there was evidence of contraband. Therefore, the dog was only disclosing criminal behavior and a warrant was not necessary. No intrusion of an innocent person's privacy would occur.

But what of the question of accuracy? Air scent dogs are not totally accurate. The question then is whether the dog's alert *by itself* constitutes probable cause to obtain a warrant. One can reach two possible conclusions. First, a well-trained dog may make a mistake, but is sufficiently accurate to meet the test for obtaining a warrant. The second conclusion would require independent, corroborative evidence in order for a warrant to be justified.

Another issue involves a dog alerting outside an area that is considered private and subject to the constraints of the fourth amendment. Does the alert of a trained dog outside a certain apartment allow officers to enter and search the apartment? The Supreme Court answered "no" in the case of Thomas. The court reasoned that the use of the dog was an invasion of a private space. The dog gave the police information that they could not otherwise derive. Mr. Thomas had a legitimate expectation that his apartment would remain private and that what went on inside could not be "sensed" through his closed door.

The court distinguished Thomas from the case of Colyer. The difference was that Colyer was on a train in a sleeper compartment. The court concluded that a sleeper compartment in a train lacked the "heightened privacy interest" found in a house or apartment. The room in the train was felt to be similar to an automobile.

The above examples indicate that the issue of what constitutes a search can be difficult to discern. Clearly the activities of an air scent dog are less intrusive than many other searches. The Supreme Court has held that a limited, warrantless search can occur with less than full probable cause. This is the holding of Terry *v.* Ohio. Terry allows a balance between the need to search and the degree of invasion a search entails. An air scent dog searching for drugs, explosives, accelerants, etc., is a lesser intrusion and so may be subject to lesser fourth amendment restrictions. Currently the Supreme Court appears loathe to extend Terry beyond searches for weapons, or when there are "special needs" searches.

Many courts have allowed searches by air scent dogs without a warrant when the search has been based on other facts that gave the police a reasonable suspicion. Courts, however, will not allow dogs to be used for general exploratory or dragnet type searches. The decisions in these cases appear to be very fact-specific. The court's decision to allow lesser evidence or exigent circumstances to be substituted for the need to obtain a warrant remains unpredictable.

The issues discussed above rarely occur in the context of cadaver dog searches. These searches usually are the result of prior investigation. Cadaver searches by their very nature will lack exigent circumstances except in the rarest cases. Those cases will usually involve the suspicion that a vehicle either has a body in it or was used to transport a body.

The principal area of concern for cadaver dog handlers is the possibility of warrantless entry onto property where there is a justified expectation of privacy. These places would include a person's home, place of business, vehicle, possessions, and his or her person. In the State *v.* Mooney (218 Conn. 85), a 1991 decision, the protection was extended to the area where a homeless person sleeps and keeps his or her belongings. Unconsented entry into motel and hotel rooms constitutes a search requiring a warrant under the Fourth Amendment. Businesses are also subject to Fourth Amendment restrictions, though law enforcement officers may enter those areas that are open to the public and to which the public has ready access. The use of a cadaver dog in non-public locations requires either a warrant or the consent of the owner/tenant.

Open fields are not protected by the Fourth Amendment. The U.S. Supreme Court decided this in the case of Hester. This view has been upheld in later cases. The concept of open fields extends to any unoccupied or undeveloped area which may be neither "open" or "a field." Certainly it would apply to woods, swamps, desert, etc. The apparent reasoning is that an individual cannot expect or demand privacy for activities occurring out of doors except in the area immediately surrounding the dwelling.

Between a residence and the surrounding "open fields" lies the *curtilage* (see Figure 6.1). The curtilage is that area adjacent to a structure in which an individual has an expectation of privacy to which society is in agreement. The search of curtilage requires a warrant or consent. Courts usually look to four factors when determining the protected area. The first of these is the proximity of the area to the residence or business. Second, one looks to see whether there is an enclosure such as a fence or hedge. The third factor is the use to which the area is put. Finally, courts will evaluate the steps taken by the owner to ensure privacy and restrict visibility to the passing public. Curtilage also includes outbuildings, if these buildings are used in connection with the primary residence. Thus, a barn or shed will be considered within the curtilage if there is evidence of a connection. This connection may be a path or drive connecting the structures. It may be that the structure is surrounded by the same perimeter fence as the residence. Distance is not the chief factor. An outbuilding separated from the residence by a fence or other obstruction (natural or man-made) will be considered outside the curtilage even if it is in close proximity.

Public land may be searched without a warrant as there are no individual privacy issues invloved. This would include all land open to the public, including federal, state, and municipal parks and forests, and the rights of way for highways.

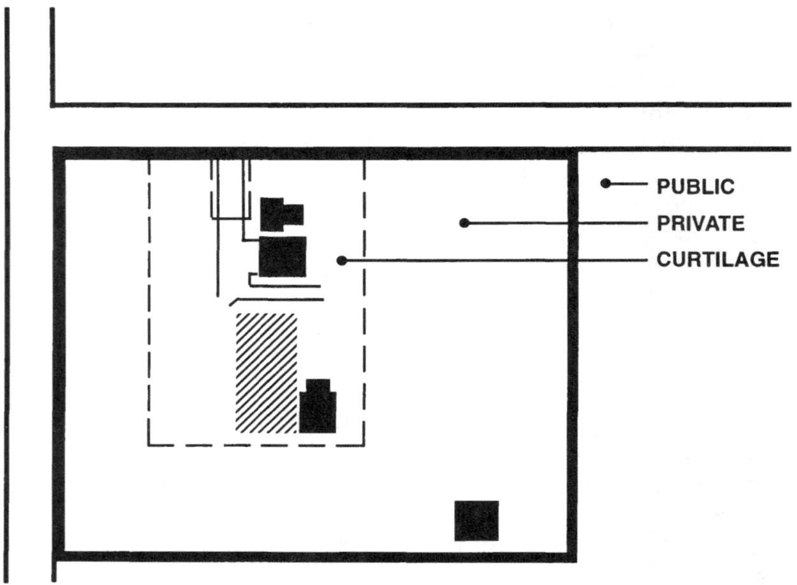

Figure 6.1 Curtilage

Sufficient showing as to the reliability of a cadaver dog for the detection of human remains must be made if the alert of that dog is going to be used as probable cause for the issuance of either an arrest or search warrant. Issues that will be looked at include the training of both the dog and the handler, the standards employed in the selecting and training of dogs, the standards that the dog had to meet before being allowed to search, the ongoing training of the dog, and a record of the dog's searches including both positive and false alerts.

A reasonable search, then, is one based on probable cause. How does this affect a dog handler involved in a search? Very simply, if a handler is not legally entitled to be in a location, and he or she find pertinent evidence, any resulting testimony or evidence will be suppressed in court.

Substantial evidence in two areas is necessary for a search warrant to be issued. It must be shown that the item sought is connected to a criminal activity and also that it is in the place to be searched. Probable cause represents an accommodation between the constitutional right of privacy and effective law enforcement. Some courts have extended this balance of interest and process by looking at the intrusiveness of a search. Where intrusiveness has been weighed, searches by dogs are generally considered to be less intrusive than other means. The alert of a dog can then lead to a second warrant to allow digging or other necessary invasion into the area alerted upon.

The constitutional requirements for a search warrant follow:

1. It must describe, with particularity, the place to be searched.
2. It must describe, with particularity, the items to be seized.
3. It must be based on probable cause.
4. It must be supported by a sworn affidavit.
5. It must be issued by a neutral and detached magistrate.

A search warrant must be executed within 10 days of its issuance and a copy of the warrant must be given to the owner or occupant of the property that is searched. A return on the warrant, including an inventory of all property seized, must be filed with the court with reasonable promptness.

There are certain exceptions to the requirement for a search warrant:

- *Plain view* requires that the officer be in a position where he or she can view the object lawfully and that the object is believed to be contraband, stolen property, or evidence of a crime.
- *Consent search* requires that written or verbal consent be obtained to conduct the search. Consent should be obtained in writing.
- *Exigent circumstances* asserts that police are allowed to enter premises and conduct searches without a search warrant in situations where they have reason to believe that a failure to search will lead to destruction or concealment of evidence, injury to the officers or others, or the escape of a suspect. Such entry should be made only when they believe they have insufficient time to obtain a warrant.

The authority for the search is noted in a search warrant. *The scene investigation is, thus, directed not by the handler/dog team, but by a person representing either law enforcement or the coroner/ medical examiner.* The cadaver dog team must report to that person before, during, and after the search. Such coordination, along with proper documentation and handling of evidence (including chain of custody documentation) is necessary to prevent evidence found during the search from being suppressed in court. The handler should discuss the search strategy with the authorized scene investigator prior to its implementation. If a change in strategy is necessary, this needs to be communicated before it is carried out.

As mentioned above, the remedy for an improper search is to exclude the evidence gathered during that search. This is the "Exclusionary Rule." The Exclusionary Rule is not expressly stated in the Fourth

Amendment. To allow illegally seized evidence to be admitted would give approval to unconstitutional conduct. The Exclusionary Rule extends not only to the evidence initially seized, but to any evidence subsequently seized because of that initial illegal act. This is the "Fruit of the Poisonous Tree" doctrine. It is therefore critical that a proper search warrant exist before entering into a search where criminal activity is suspected.

The court must decide whether the expert testimony to be given (in this case by the handler) will be of assistance to the trier of fact. The court must then determine whether the witness is properly qualified to give testimony on the basis of knowledge, skill, experience, training, education, or a combination of these. It is also important for the court to know if other courts have granted expert standing to a canine/handler team.

The court frequently is also required to determine whether there is a sufficiently reliable body of knowledge surrounding an area of (expert) testimony to allow it in as evidence. Prior to the U.S. Supreme Court's decision in Daubert *v.* Merrill-Dow Pharmaceuticals Inc. (509 U.S. 579, 113 5. Ct. 2786 (1993)), the Court used a general acceptance threshold known as the Frye test. The Daubert decision has replaced the Frye test in federal courts with the language of Federal Rule of Evidence 702 (FRE 702). Many states have also adopted the Daubert approach. Daubert requires that expert testimony reflect scientific knowledge derived by scientific method. It requires the court to act as a gatekeeper and determine whether the science is "good," that is, relevant, testable, and subject to peer review.

All evidence, whether expert testimony or not, is subject to Federal Rule of Evidence 403 (FRE 403) or its state counterpart. FRE 403 requires a balancing between the *probative value* of evidence (its ability to prove/disprove) and the prejudice it may engender. The probative value must substantially outweigh an unfair prejudice. The issues of admissibility under the rules of evidence are most commonly decided prior to trial through such activities such as motions to suppress.

This discussion points to the importance of developing accepted procedures to evaluate and certify reliability of particular dog/handler teams, as well as the importance of research to demonstrate the scientific basis of the method in general. It also underscores the critical nature of good documentation, including careful description and interpretation of search contexts, techniques, and results.

PRACTICAL IMPLICATIONS FOR CANINE SEARCHES IN GENERAL

What effects do the warrant requirements have on the conduct of a canine search? It depends on the type of search and under what circumstances it is conducted.

The guidelines for searches with a tracking or trailing dog differ from those that govern a search for evidence or for human remains. In the former instance, the track may lead to a private residence. If the owner or occupant denies access, a decision must be made whether to gain immediate entry or apply for a warrant to enter and search for a person, evidence, etc.

The decision regarding entry should be based on the type of crime, the amount of time that has elapsed since the commission of the crime, and whether the suspect might harm others or flee. It is always preferable to proceed under the authority of a search warrant.

The actions of the tracking/trailing dog may be used as a portion of the probable cause for the search warrant. There are numerous legal precedents for the inclusion of tracking dog performance in warrant applications.

The documentation of experience and training of the handler and dog are not as stringent for a warrant application as those required for court testimony. The warrant should give a description of the actions of the dog on a trail, including the type of scent material, path traveled, and opinion of the handler that the dog was following a valid track. A brief summary of handler experience, how long he or she has worked with the particular dog, that the dog is trained to discriminate scents, and previous cases where the dog was worked should be sufficient.

A missing person search is frequently considered a search under exigent circumstances. The incident is often considered an emergency because of the circumstances surrounding the disappearance and concern for the health and welfare of the victim. The search area is covered thoroughly, including yards and outbuildings in the vicinity of private residences, especially when the search is for a small child or disoriented elderly person.

IMPLICATIONS FOR CADAVER DOG SEARCHES

A cadaver search on private property should be conducted only under the authority of a search warrant or a written consent to search from the owner or occupant of the property. The warrant application should not only specify that the search is an attempt to locate the body, but also should specify weapons, hairs, fibers, blood, and other items of evidence. The application must specify exactly the property to be searched.

Most speculative searches for human remains originate from an informant, and it is the responsibility of the investigator to assess the reliability of the information. A search with a trained dog for human remains is generally considered a *non-intrusive search*. The courts may regard such a search favorably, whereas an application to dig up the property with a backhoe based on the same information may be denied.

It is important that the stipulations set forth in the warrant be followed. During one homicide investigation, a search warrant was obtained for the suspect's vehicle. Once the warrant was issued, the vehicle was towed from the residence to the troop garage, where the vehicle was checked by a dog for possible body fluids. The dog alerted in the trunk and forensic processing located physical evidence. The judge refused to allow testimony regarding the evidence into the trial, because the address for the search was listed as the residence, not the troop garage.

The reverse is also true. The dog can be used to check a vehicle and a warrant can be issued for another location based on the dog's actions. For example, while investigating a possible suicide in Vermont, the missing person's car was found in a rural area on a dirt road. The vehicle was towed to the barracks for safe keeping. In the meantime, search dogs were used to search the area, with negative results.

When the search team returned to the barracks, they entered through the garage, with the dog at a heel. Two detectives were doing an inventory of the victim's vehicle and as the search team passed by, the dog alerted on the trunk, which was cracked open. When the trunk was opened further, the dog jumped in, scratching at the carpet. The dog was then used to check the car completely; she also alerted on the floor of the passenger compartment. When the two areas were checked by the forensic laboratory, type B human blood was identified. Since the missing person had type B blood, the dog's alert changed the focus of the investigation.

The property where the missing person lived was a farm, which he had recently transferred to new owners. But he was temporarily living on the premises. The new owners had originally allowed the police to check his bedroom, however they denied them further access. Using the information developed from the dog's alert, a search warrant was obtained. The premises were checked with the dog. The dog alerted on an area on the stairs from the victim's bedroom, which was spotted with blood. In this situation, further access to the residence probably would not have been possible without a warrant. A warrant would have been difficult to obtain without the aid of the dog, since, initially, foul play was not suspected.

During a search for a possible kidnap victim, the police developed a possible suspect who resided adjacent to property owned by a water company. Consent was obtained for a speculative search of the water company property. The dog alerted on windborn scent and located a body in thick overgrowth off an old logging road. The victim was on land owned by a private party, not the property where investigators had permission to search. The area was secured until the proper permission was obtained, thereby preserving the admissibility of any physical evidence.

The police officer in charge of the investigation is responsible for the legality of the search; however, K-9 handlers should also be aware of the requirements for conducting a legal search. In the past, comments have been raised by volunteer search and rescue (SAR) dog handlers about the conduct of a search. In one instance, a search for a missing woman was being conducted where she had last been seen. Information was developed that implicated a party who lived several miles from the search scene, and investigators went to the home to question him. A K-9 handler suggested to investigators that the area around his house be searched, and was upset when he was turned down. If the officer in charge of the investigation and search had explained that enough probable cause did not exist to allow a legal search, the misunderstanding between the police and SAR dog handlers would have been cleared up.

Remember, if any question exists about the propriety of conducting a search, it is always better to obtain legal authority than have important evidence be suppressed at a trial.

CHAPTER 7

HANDLING A SEARCH REQUEST

RECORD KEEPING REGARDING REQUESTS

We recommend that you keep a record of any search request. This should include the date and contact person, as well as information about the case. There are several responses possible for a request:

- Search appears feasible and is implemented
- Search appears feasible, but you and your dog are unable to implement due to scheduling problems or lack of training for a particular type of search; you may refer the case to a colleague
- Search appears problematic; you explore potential difficulties with the client up front before deciding to proceed. It is important for the client to be aware of any limitations due to the site, the weather, your dog, or your training
- Search is not feasible; you inform the client of the difficulties

EVALUATING THE FEASIBILITY OF THE SEARCH

The dog handler will need some preliminary information in order to evaluate the feasibility of the search and to formulate a search plan. The plan will specify the number of teams needed and the time frame required for the search.

Depending on the type of search, the information should include the following items:

1. Type of case—homicide, suicide, missing person, etc.
2. Location of the search area
3. How the search area is being defined
4. How many victims are involved
5. How well the suspects know the area and possible hiding places
6. If the request is a result of informant information, what the agency's assessment is of the reliability of the information

7. How long the victim has been missing
8. The time of year the victim disappeared, the general temperature at that time (e.g., if there was a substantial amount of frost in the ground, digging would have been difficult)
9. If the victim was walked, carried, or dragged to the site
10. The time of day/night the body was buried (e.g., limitations that would place on the suspects' efforts)
11. What search efforts have already been conducted
12. What type of terrain exists in the search area and whether there have been any changes (e.g., construction or earth moving) since the victim disappeared
13. If investigators suspect the victim was buried, the general type of soil in the area
14. What position the body was buried in
15. The size of the search area and whether there are any other areas that should be searched if the primary search area proves negative
16. Whether the agency wants the search to be low profile (e.g., whether the handlers should wear civilian clothing and vehicles should be unmarked)
17. If the search involves private property, whether the agency has obtained either a written consent to search or a search warrant

EVALUATING THE APPROPRIATENESS OF USING A PARTICULAR HANDLER OR CANINE

There are several training characteristics that impact the choice of dog/handler team. Some dogs are trained and experienced with burials or with surface finds, and sometimes not both. Some dogs are experienced with particular types of searches, but not others, e.g., vehicle searches, indoors searches, wilderness searches. It is best not to put the dog and/or handler into a new search situation with inadequate training. Handlers that receive requests for types of searches that they have not trained for are advised to refer the case to a more appropriate team. Failures due to inexperience or lack of training will only damage the reputation of a team in the long run.

SCHEDULING A SEARCH: SEASON, TIME, WEATHER

It is important to be realistic about environmental conditions. Schedule a search at a time that maximizes the probability of success.

Searches in freezing temperatures or during times of significant snow cover are compromised from the outset. In most cases it is better to wait for warmer weather or for the snow to melt.

Try to schedule searches for morning or afternoon, but avoid the midday. The air currents are much more active early and late in the day.

Avoid beginning searches late in the day. Darkness is not only inhibitory for locating remains, it is potentially dangerous. Even experienced handlers can become lost and disoriented.

PROMISES AND DELIVERABLES

Be realistic about the barriers to success (see also Chapter 5, Levels of Certainty). Excessive optimism will reduce credibility in the long run. For example, assuring clients that buried remains can always be found, or that any remains deposited under 30 years ago (or any other such time frame) will certainly be found by your dogs is unrealistic at best. Use phrases such as "has a good likelihood of being found, if it is there" for cases with a high probability of success. But use phrases such as "there are a number of factors that reduce the chances of success" for cases with lower probability. Educate your potential clients about the limitations and pitfalls. Explain about differential environmental conditions, variability in weather conditions, and variability in terrain.

We have found that, despite the best efforts of investigators, a majority of searches in fact have negative results. In most cases, this is because the remains simply are not there. In these cases, the best that can be done is "rule out" an area—with varying degrees of probability. Never 100 percent. You can conclude that "there is a high probability the remains are not there," but avoid statements that might lead investigators to assume there is no doubt. Particularly if the wind conditions are not very favorable during your search, or if you decide to avoid searching selected areas difficult to access, search conclusions need to include honest statements of limitation.

It is tempting to be optimistic and to promote the efficacy of cadaver dogs. It is tempting to be quiet about limitations or errors in the search. But cadaver dog searching is far from an exact science. Handlers make errors. Dogs become fatigued or have bad days. Environmental conditions distort the scent picture. Realistic assessment and realistic expectations are the best road to promoting cadaver dogs in the long run.

WHEN TO SAY NO

Some proposed search areas are not feasible for search by the K-9 team. A prime example is a landfill where waste materials are deposited on a regular basis. The site is normally compacted as often as daily, contains an abundance of decaying organic matter, and may contain hazardous materials, posing a danger to the dog and handler.

CHAPTER 8

THE SEARCH

INTRODUCTION

Developing and executing a successful search strategy depends on a broad range of variables, including the type of search, the terrain, the type of circumstances leading to the death, and the time since death. All of these characteristics interact to make each search unique. Until the handler arrives at the scene, it is impossible to make decisions about the search strategy. In fact, although the success of any search ultimately depends on the dog and its training, the intellectual challenge resides with the handler. It is the handler who directs (and redirects) the dog. It is quite possible, for example, for a handler to prevent a dog from working a scent cone correctly, or to direct it in such a way that the scent cannot be detected because of the combination of wind direction and dog direction.

Several types of errors are possible:

- The body is present, but the dog never entered the scent cone due to wind direction, scent cone distortion, or faulty search structure
- The dog entered the scent cone, but the handler failed to recognize key behaviors
- The dog entered the scent cone, but was too tired or poorly trained to give its indication

It is necessary for the handler to have a comprehensive conceptual framework, and an understanding of the theoretical issue in order to solve the problems connected with each search. In this and the next chapter we present an overview of these basic search concepts.

We have defined a canine cadaver search as "the investigation of a particular area deemed by forensic investigators to contain human remains according to a strategy designed for that particular context" (Sorg, David, and Rebmann, 1998, p. 124). It is possible that multiple searches may be required to investigate a single death. Conversely, a single investigation of an heterogeneous area may require several searches. A single search may take minutes, days, or weeks.

TYPES OF CANINE CADAVER SEARCHES

There are three major canine cadaver search types, defined based on the impetus for the search. These three types each require a different approach, particularly a different orientation to the scent cone.

RECOVERY EXPANSION SEARCH

In a recovery expansion search, remains have already been discovered in a particular area. The goal may be to locate additional, possibly scattered, remains. Or it may be necessary to identify locations where the body had been prior to being scattered or moved. With this first search type, the location of one or more scent cones is already known. If the area where the discovery was made was well-searched, these are the lowest priority for searching. On the other hand, the scatter pattern of remains already found may provide the best information about where to direct the next search. For example, the search strategy may focus on animal trails, areas of higher ground, or on hypothetical areas implied by the anatomical distribution of the scatter pattern. It is necessary to know what remains were found in which locations, as well as the likelihood of unfound remains being disarticulated (either by decomposition or animal chewing) and fragmented. Keep in mind that even areas that previously have been cleared can produce remains due to intervening animal activity.

In a recovery expansion search there are two typical scenarios:

- Remains have been scattered by animals, explosion, or other agents and only part of the body has been found. These bodies may have been originally buried or on the surface. (The decomposition scent is usually detectable by scavengers and by cadaver dogs when the burial is less than two feet deep.) In such cases it will be important to have an ongoing inventory of remains found in order to know when the job is done. It is also important to locate where the body was originally placed, even if the body is gone, so that spot can be examined for other evidence.
- Remains have been discovered in one location and there is a question about whether they have been moved from another location within that same area.

If remains previously have been in a given location and removed either by animals or by a recovery operation, the scent cones will still be present. Decomposition scent will have seeped into the area surrounding the body location. In fact, there may be many potentially overlapping and confusing scent cones in a specific area. If the fragmentation is profound, as with a plane crash, for example, the scent may literally be everywhere at once, presenting an overwhelming scent "picture" to the dog. It will take the dog a while to become oriented to subtle differences in scent intensity.

In a case where the postmortem interval is short, decomposition odor is strong, and recovery recent, the dog may alert in locations where remains have already been removed. Hopefully, these locations will have been flagged so the handler knows there is scent there even though there are no remains, and can reward the dog. Alerting to previously removed remains is to be expected, and can even be encouraged. In this way the dog initially "discovers" the scent sources, and can be rewarded; this improves motivation.

In areas where there is scatter, it may be helpful to direct the dog to perform a preliminary perimeter search, sometimes also called a hasty or scanning search. This preliminary overview will give the dog an overall sensory picture, allowing it to focus on areas of more intensity and interest.

FOCUSED SPECULATIVE SEARCH

In this search type, investigative work has focused attention on a particular area where the remains are suspected to be, with the boundaries fairly well defined. There are one or more scent cone sources suspected, and these are generally the highest priority for searching. These may be areas identified by informants, or suspicious places suggested by the investigation. The goal is to either locate the remains or "clear" the area.

An example of such a search is a suspected suicide. Areas where the missing person was known to go regularly, particularly favorite outdoor spots, may be targeted for searching. Similarly, a suspected homicide may involve searching a basement or a yard near a particular dwelling.

Generally the search will begin at the site itself, or downwind of it. If no remains are found, the search may be expanded using a spiral or radial search pattern. It is particularly important not to over-direct the dog; the handler should treat the area neutrally while ensuring that the search is thorough.

In some cases the information source is known to be unreliable, but the area must be ruled out. In these situations the handler should avoid any temptation to rush or cut corners. Depending on wind direction, it may not be possible to clear the entire area. For example, in doing a search focused on a meadow bordered by a wooded area which is downwind, it may not be possible to clear the downwind edge of the meadow without entering the woods. Each search should be described objectively, with limitations explicitly stated, even when the (negative) results confirm expectations.

NON-FOCUSED SPECULATIVE SEARCHES

Often the team is asked to search a more general area, with the boundaries not well-defined. The goals of a non-focused speculative search should be developed clearly, in collaboration with investigators. Usually, when the perimeter is unclear, an arbitrary boundary will need to be set. This can be based on a combination of characteristics, such as the area that can be searched in one day, the wind direction, or the terrain and likelihood of access by the victim or perpetrator.

Obviously, the goal in this type of search is to find the scent cone. But the cone is only hypothetical from the point of view of the handler (who cannot smell it). So, once the arbitrary perimeter and focus is agreed upon, the search generally is commenced perpendicular to the wind direction. Frequently, in outdoor searches, attention will be given to the sides or terminal points of paths or roads. Conversely, wide open spaces may be searched with an overall grid pattern.

There are no perfect searches. The handler needs to stay alert to possible scent cone distortions, compensate as necessary, but let the dog do the ultimate problem solving. During the search, weather conditions may change causing the search to be altered or postponed, or resulting in one area having better coverage than another. Some areas may not be searched due to potential dangers to dog or handler. Following each effort, careful attention should be paid to describing the attempt, including the weather conditions, search strategy, results, and the strengths and weaknesses.

Each search's success should be evaluated within its unique context. A search may fail to locate a victim, but still be a success. As we have itemized previously (Sorg, David and Rebmann, 1998) there are several reasons for a failure to locate human remains:

- The missing person is not dead
- The body is not in that location
- The body was moved (or scattered) from that location
- The body's scent is inaccessible to the dog due to weather or terrain
- The dog or handler is inadequately trained and the handler missed the dog's alert or the dog failed to alert correctly
- The search strategy was not appropriate to weather, terrain, or investigative information
- The recovery strategy was not appropriate

Some factors, such as the quality of the investigative work and the recovery effort in areas indicated by the dog, are beyond the handler's control. But the handler can act to ensure good training, good communication with investigators, careful scheduling of the search to take advantage of weather and light and area to be searched, and appropriate interpretation and documentation of search results.

FORENSIC CONTEXTS

The tactics used for a cadaver search are basically the same as those employed for wilderness search. However, since the search area may be large and the amount of available scent small compared to the volume emitted by a live person, the handler must give careful attention to planning the search to provide the maximum probability of detection.

There are several, relatively common forensic contexts, each requiring a different approach. They include the following:

Homicide—unpremeditated
Homicide—premeditated
Homicide—serial murder
Suicide
Missing person: elderly with dementia

To assist in planning, you need to understand some of the basic behavioral patterns of the actor/perpetrator and how the behavior may affect the method of disposal of a body. The sophistication involved in the means of disposal in homicides depends to a great extent upon the psychological makeup of the killer and the circumstances of the crime.

UNPREMEDITATED HOMICIDE

An unpremeditated or accidental homicide usually results from an argument escalating to physical violence. The perpetrator, when the reality of his actions sinks in, wants to dispose of the body as rapidly as possible, hoping the crime will go undetected. Since he is almost in a panic, he will normally spend very little time disposing of the corpse.

Many of these victims are dumped from a vehicle along a roadside or in a rural area such as a lover's lane. There may be an attempt made to conceal the body in thick growth or by covering it with brush, leaves or debris. If the perpetrator attempts to bury the victim, the grave usually is shallow (6-24 inches), hastily dug, and sloppily refilled.

When questioned, the suspect will frequently lead the investigators to the corpse or the general area. Occasionally, if the disposal was done at night, he may not be able to identify the exact area. If the suspect has provided general landmarks, the probable search areas can be identified. If the landmarks fit several locations, the search area increases.

PREMEDITATED HOMICIDE

The actor in a premeditated homicide takes the time to plan the circumstances of the crime, including the disposal of the corpse. He may even dig the grave prior to committing the crime. He will normally select a location where he feels comfortable and is confident that he will be undisturbed and can come and go without being noticed. The grave may be deeper, and the suspect may take the time to make sure there is no physical sign of the grave site.

SERIAL MURDERS

The serial murderer is a special classification of criminal. There are multiple victims over a period of time, ranging from months to years. Methods of disposal vary, from multiple victims buried in one general area to disposal over a large geographical area.

Many serial murder victims are merely discarded in a wooded area, with little or no attempt to bury or otherwise conceal the body. The existence of the serial killer becomes apparent when the bodies of several victims are discovered and a pattern emerges in the method of disposal and circumstances of death. Many times the victims have similar backgrounds or physical characteristics.

Through an analysis of the disposal sites, a profile of the "typical" potential site can be developed. If there are a number of reported missing persons, matching characteristics and who disappeared under similar circumstances as the discovered victims, the profile areas can be searched for possible additional victims. There may be a large number of sites that fit the profile within the geographical area the killer frequents.

SEARCH PARAMETERS

Parameters that can be used to define search areas for homicide victims follow:

- The body will normally be within a 100 yard radius of an area accessible by a vehicle.
- The remains will normally be on the same level or downgrade from the parking area.
- If buried, the grave will generally be between 6 and 24 inches deep. The site may be disguised with brush, leaves, or debris.

There are a number of documented cases where the killer has returned to the disposal site after a period of time and removed the remains. This has occurred when he fears that information may have been given to the authorities by an informant, which would lead to the discovery of the remains. The cadaver dog may be able to identify the area. Careful processing of the scene may provide evidence that the body had previously been at the location.

One thing to consider is the possibility that the perpetrator may participate in the initial search for the victim. He may be a volunteer searcher or offer suggestions to the search manager regarding probable search areas.

Many of the searches for homicide victims are speculative. You may search for hours without locating anything. A speculative search results when the investigators have sketchy information from an informant or are playing a hunch.

Never take a speculative search lightly. Many have resulted with the discovery of a homicide victim. The most difficult part of conducting a speculative search is maintaining the handler's optimism and the working efficiency of the dog.

SUICIDE

The cadaver dog is a common resource used to locate a suicide victim. It is a generally accepted theory that there are two basic types of suicide. The first type desires to be found. These individuals will generally be in the residence, in a vehicle, or within a short distance from the residence or vehicle.

The individual who does not want to be found may pose a challenge to the dog team. They may crawl under a windfall, enter the water, or hang themselves from an evergreen tree at a height where the body may be difficult to see.

A suicide victim is generally within a one-quarter mile radius of the last known location. In many instances they are at a high place where they can find solitude. When the possible suicide victim has consumed a combination of alcoholic beverages and pills near a watercourse, the highest probability location will be in the water.

ELDERLY PERSONS SUFFERING FROM DEMENTIA

It is extremely difficult to predict a behavior pattern for these subjects. They are disoriented and are easily confused. In many instances they appear to wander aimlessly. In wooded areas, they frequently leave paths and enter thick, almost impenetrable brush. We have located victims who have crawled into a place of shelter or have covered themselves with brush and leaves before they expired. Many are reported to have difficulty walking (they only shuffle); however, they frequently travel long distances and navigate extremely rough terrain.

PHYSICAL CONTEXTS

Cadaver searches can take place wherever people can travel or take a body. They can take place inside a closed area such as a building or car, or outdoors. If outdoors, they can take place on land, on water, or in a combination of settings. The outdoor scenes can be in residential, industrial, or wilderness areas. Because of the extreme variation in physical contexts, it will be important to do as much careful planning as possible. It will also be important to have a repertoire of search tactics and standard operating procedures to call upon in order to ensure good coverage and consistent results.

USE OF TECHNICAL LOCATION AND MAPPING AIDS

AIDS TO LOCATION

The purpose of a search is to locate something. To do that one must know where he is, where he is going and, when located, the position of the find. As detailed in other chapters, searches vary in the degree of probability that something will be found. We have characterized these searches as being either "focused" or "unfocused." Searches are also characterized as "speculative" or not. Additionally, the area to be searched can dictate the usefulness of a dog versus other remote sensing modalities. This section will discuss the use of maps, compass, global positioning satellite receivers, human sensory search clues, and other remote sensing techniques. The following tasks are often part of the search:

- Document the location and boundaries of the planned search
- Plan for variations in terrain and vegetation
- Document location and boundaries of the actual search
- Document location and boundaries of "cleared" area
- Increase the confidence in "clearing" an area
- Enable return to exact location of area for further searching
- Document location of evidence or remains found
- Interpret pattern of scattered remains

Maps

Maps vary greatly in detail. A hand-drawn sketch of the area to be searched lies at one extreme. Detailed topographic maps are at the other extreme. Either one when properly oriented allows searchers to take a bearing and to orient themselves within the search area. The discussion below will focus on topographic maps. References will be to maps and map software programs covering the United States.

A topographic map utilizes contour lines to inform the user of a three-dimensional landscape on a two-dimensional surface. Familiarity with a topographic map allows one to view the landscape in three dimensions. The contour lines, generally printed in brown, vary in width and indicate changes in elevation. The wider the spacing the more gradual the change in elevation. Other frequently used colors include green (for vegetation), blue (for water), white (for open terrain), and black (for man-made features including buildings and roads).

Topographic maps are available from a wide variety of sources. The standard is that produced by the United States Geological Survey (U.S.G.S.). It is important to note that these maps may not have been revised for many years. One should always check the revision date on the map. Obviously the greatest chance for error lies with man-made structures, most critically roads. Topographic maps are also privately produced by companies such as DeLorme. These maps tend to have less detail than those produced by the U.S.G.S.

Recently, companies such as DeLorme and Maptech have begun to produce map programs on CD-ROM for computer use. The Maptech programs actually are U.S.G.S. topographic maps. Not all areas of the country are available from all companies. One of the more useful functions available on some of the programs is the ability to directly download global positioning satellite (GPS) information.

When using any map it is critical to understand the scale and the meaning of the various symbols. This information is usually found on the border of the map. U.S.G.S. maps do not contain a legend. This information is available separately. A U.S.G.S. map will contain information regarding when it was last updated, the scale, the datum used and the quadrant designation. The border will also give the names of the adjacent quadrants.

Scale is critical to using any map. Most hand-drawn maps will lack scale. They will rely on prominent features to aid the user. Most other maps will have a bar scale that will allow for distance measurements. The bar scale will also give the user an idea of the total area covered and so the detail conveyed by the map. U.S.G.S. maps are printed in two series. Most common is the 7.5-minute series. Some 15-minute series maps are still available. The minute nomenclature derives from the fact that the earth is divided into 360 degrees, with each degree further divided into 60 minutes, and each minute into 60 seconds. A 7.5-minute series map scales to 1:24,000. This means that one unit of measurement on the map equals 24,000 units of measurement on the ground.

Multiple bearing systems have been developed and are in use in various parts of the world. Among the more popular are Maidenhead, Ordnance Survey of Great Britain, and Trimble Atlas. The two generally in use in the United States are "latitude and longitude" and "universal transverse mercator." Most maps will have changes in degrees, minutes, and seconds of latitude along the right and the left border of the map. The latitude increases as one goes north from the equator. Maps may omit degrees if their scale is not large enough to have a change in degrees. Longitude is indicated along the top and bottom of the map. Longitude increases has one goes from east to west.

Universal transverse mercator (UTM) has its major use when using the GPS system. The UTM system divides the world into 60, 6 degree zones. The zones begin and end at 180 degrees east-west longitude. Each zone is removed from the globe and flattened. This causes distortion because of the loss of relationship to the spherical shape. Above 84 degrees north latitude and 80 degrees south latitude this distortion is of such severity that UTM cannot be used. The UTM system is metric and one kilometer separates each grid line. North-south positions are found on the right and left side of the map. East-west positions are found along the top and bottom of the map. Some of the maps will put the markings along only one horizontal and one vertical margin. The vertical markings are called "northings" and the horizontal markings are called "eastings." Increasing northing numbers indicate one is heading north. Decreasing northing numbers indicate a southerly direction. Increasing easting numbers indicate one is heading east, while decreasing numbers indicate a westerly direction. The numbering system consists of two full-size numbers, three small numbers superiorly, a small "m" and either a capital "E" or "N" (example: $^{6}44^{000}$m.N).

Compasses

Two pieces of equipment can tell you where you are and can get you to where you want to go. They are a compass and a GPS receiver. It is the authors' opinion that skill with a compass is critical. Compass knowledge can be transferred easily to navigating with the GPS unit. The converse is not true. Also a compass does not require batteries, a source of possible failure in the field.

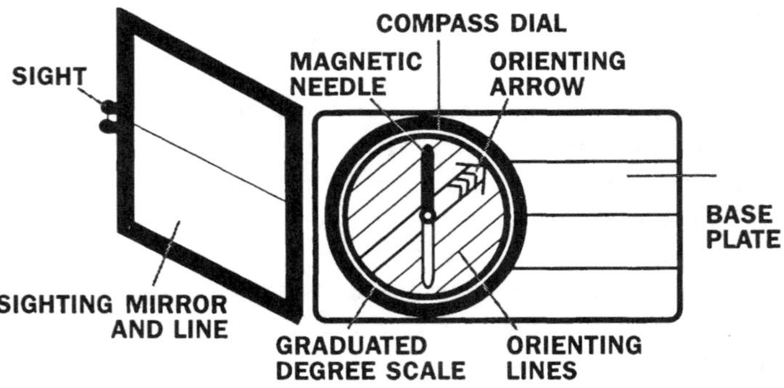

Figure 8.1 Basic mirror compass

There are multiple types of compasses. A mirror-sighting compass is probably the best overall choice for doing search work with a canine (Figure 8.1). This type of compass usually has two-degree increments allowing for one-degree accuracy. It will have oriented arrows, liquid damping to allow the needle to come to rest rapidly and to remain steady for accurate readings, a sighting mirror for greater accuracy and declination correction scales. The baseplate will have inch and millimeter scales. It is human nature to doubt one's compass. It should not be considered overkill to carry two compasses. Rarely, a compass will fail. More problematic is the possibility of iron inappropriately deviating the needle. Having a second compass can reassure the handler.

It is perhaps worthwhile to discuss declination. The difference between true north shown on a topographic map and magnetic north as indicated by the compass needle is known as declination. U.S.G.S. topographic maps will show the declination. There will be two arrows forming an angle. The longer arrow with a star at the top indicates true north. The shorter arrow with "MN" indicates magnetic north. A compass with declination correction allows you to turn a screw so that the compass reads true. One should always check declination particularly if called to a different part of the country for a search.

Global Positioning Satellite (GPS) Receivers

Today GPS receivers are probably the most popular navigation aids. A small, handheld GPS unit provides you with your position by monitoring up to 12 of the 24 GPS system satellites in geosynchronous orbit above the earth. The satellites broadcast a radio signal based on the atomic clock, accurate to one 10 billionth of a second. The handheld receiver measures the difference in time of arrival of these signals from different satellites. This difference in time of arrival allows the receiver to calculate its position with an accuracy of within one meter. Though the U.S. Department of Defense has said they would allow this accuracy for civilian use, this has not yet happened; so, one can expect accuracy to vary between 15 meters and 100 meters depending on "selective availability." Selective availability also affects measurements of altitude. This can be critical when searching in mountainous terrain.

There is no doubt that the GPS is a valuable tool when conducting searches. It is important, however, to recognize its limitations. In addition to the signal dithering mentioned above, several other points should be remembered. First, batteries fail. This is particularly true if a search is being conducted in the cold weather. Second, to function properly the receiver must have a clear view of the sky. High cliffs, canyons and dense forest cover may block satellite signals and prevent the obtaining of a fix. GPS receivers, of course, will not work in buildings or caves.

There are two points to remember when acquiring a GPS unit. First, make sure that the unit supports the coordinate grid system that you are going to be using. It has already been mentioned that UTM is an excellent system to use with GPS. Most if not all units have both UTM and latitude-longitude. Increasingly, many other coordinate systems are available.

The second point to remember has to do with map datum. When the map is drawn the points on the map are all at a known distance and elevation from a standard reference point. This reference point is the datum. Because different maps can use a different map datum, the same location can have different coordinates! GPS has its own datum: the World Geodetic System 1984 (WGS 84). There are literally hundreds of map datums. The GPS receiver you chose must be able to translate its coordinates to those of the map datum you are using. Currently the North American Datum 1927 Continental is found on many United States maps. Some newer maps utilize North American Datum 1983. More and more United States maps will use this datum in the future.

SEARCH APPLICATIONS

Having discussed the various types of map and compass, it is time to put this information together to use it successfully in a search. Cadaver searches generally take place in an already defined area. It is not our intention in this section to teach navigation with map and compass or GPS. There are many fine books available on that subject. Rather it is our intention to make sure that after the search team is taken to the search area, that area is completely and comprehensively searched. This type of search is usually a grid or corridor search and is best conducted using a mirror-sighting compass. Since each grid will be relatively small, the declination should not present a problem.

The first thing that must be done is to orient the map to the land. Commercial maps are drawn with north at the top. Hand drawn maps may not follow this convention, so it will be necessary to identify prominent landmarks on the map and appropriately position the map. After the map has been positioned, place the compass on it and prominently indicate north by adding a hand-drawn arrow. The map and compass are now "synchronized."

Terrain and wind direction will to some degree dictate search direction. Ideally, one wants to search at 90 degrees to the prevailing wind. Obviously the absence of a prevailing wind or impassable terrain may modify that dictum.

Establish a Search Baseline and Anchor Point

The intent is to first create a search baseline (see Figure 8.2). The baseline will be at 90 degrees (perpendicular) to the route of travel/search. Prominent landmarks such as an exceptional tree, telegraph pole, or other natural feature can serve as a fixed point, anchoring the baseline. Alternatively, in urban and suburban searches, streets or buildings can serve that function. With the direction of the baseline determined by the conditions of the search, put a mark on the anchor point using tape or spray paint.

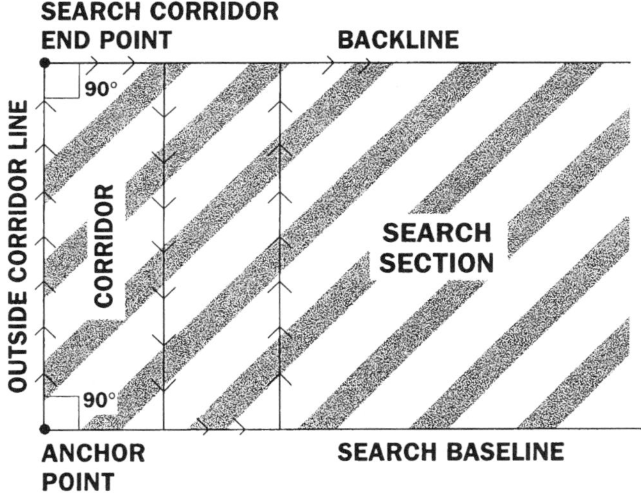

Figure 8.2 Search baseline and anchor point

Box the Compass Needle

Facing in the direction that will be traveled, hold the compass at approximately waist level, out from the body and away from any metal objects. The arrow will swing to the north and may then be "boxed" by turning the bezel until this moving arrow is overlain by the orienting arrow (the arrow engraved on the housing designed to exactly outline the magnetic needle). The direction-of-travel arrow engraved onto the base of the compass will now be followed from point to point by keeping the needle boxed within the orienting arrow (see Figure 8.3) as you proceed along the baseline.

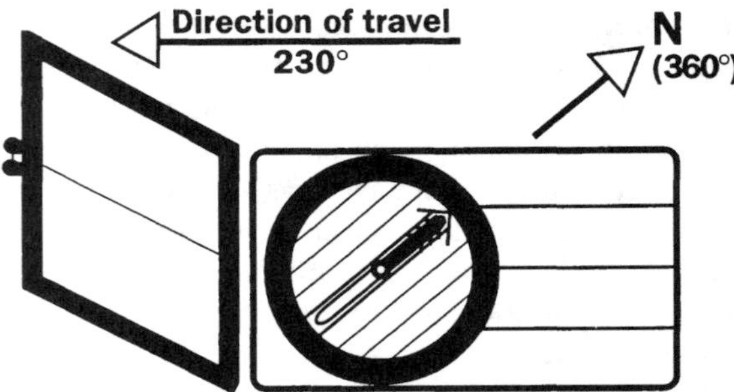

Figure 8.3 Boxing the compass needle. To take, e.g., a 230° heading, set the compass so 230° is in front of you (direction of travel). Box the compass by rotating the entire compass until the orienting arrow completely surrounds the red (north) end of the magnetic needle. Proceed in the desired direction of travel, maintaining the 230° heading by keeping the magnetic needle inside the orienting arrow

Mark the Baseline

Depending on cover, you should stop to make marks on intermediate objects along the baseline. It is a good idea to occasionally turn around 180 degrees, looking back the way you have traveled, to check progress. The fixed anchor point from which the baseline originates should be taped or marked a color different from the one marking the rest of the baseline. Markings should be visible from all sides so that the baseline will be apparent from any direction.

The length of the baseline will be determined by information leading to the search, the terrain, the number of search teams, etc. A large search having multiple teams could have a baseline as long as a mile, while a single searcher could have a baseline as small as 50 to 100 feet.

Construct the Initial Outside Corridor Line

Once the baseline is completed, return to the starting (anchor) point to construct the initial outside corridor line. This is done by standing at the anchor point, turning 90 degrees from the baseline, as measured by the compass, and then once again turning the bezel, so that the orienting arrow overlies the north-pointing compass needle. You now have a line of sight arrow at 90 degrees to baseline, and the marking procedure is performed again (as was done for the baseline).

The length of the search corridor is, again, determined by many factors, but generally will not exceed 400 yards regardless of the potential size of the search. Remember that dog and handler fatigue and interest are critical factors, and you do not want to create a search area that will exceed interest or cause fatigue.

Construct the Backline

When the initial corridor line has been completed, a suitable reference object (search corridor end point) should be marked with the same color as the baseline reference object (anchor point). The baseline and initial corridor line define two sides of a rectangular search section. Standing at the search corridor end point, turn 90 degrees, heading back in the direction of the baseline (parallel to it), and repeat the marking procedure creating the back line or perimeter of the search corridor. It is not necessary initially to go great distances along this line. Knowing the bearing, and having marked the line to a certain point, you can extend it when necessary.

Define the Corridor Width

You have now marked two right-angled arms of the search area, defining it generally, as well as a partial back line. It is now time to define the corridor width and begin searching. The search should be conducted utilizing a corridor width that meets the individual handler/dog's search pattern and ability. Some searches will occur on lead and have a corridor width of 12 feet. Other searches may be more extensive, particularly in open terrain where the dog can be seen and directed over greater distances. Some corridors may be narrower than 12 feet, as dictated by thick cover.

Begin the Search

The searcher begins at the baseline, one corridor width away from the initial corridor line, heading in a direction parallel to the initial corridor line. North is again boxed by the orienting arrow and the search progresses along the line of sight, keeping the north arrow boxed. Again, there should be frequent checks 180 degrees back to make sure you have not inadvertently wandered too far to one side or the other while circumnavigating obstacles. Periodically, flags, paint, or other markers should indicate the center line of your corridor.

When the back line is reached, an appropriate distance (one corridor width) along it is stepped off, the compass is adjusted 180 degrees, and the search returns to baseline. This procedure is continued until the entire area has been covered.

It should be noted that open terrain can present a problem. Flags, surveyor's stakes, or even untipped arrows can serve as useful makers when searching fields, etc.

As each search section is completed (when one reaches the baseline end point), the search leader should be notified so that it can be marked off on the master map. Appropriately followed, this method will allow for a complete search to be carried out. It will also allow other teams to reproduce a search of the same area.

Document Alerts and Finds

When an alert or find is made during the search, it will be necessary to pinpoint the area. Again, special flagging or paint should be used so that the find will stand out. There are two ways to appropriately designate the find spot. The first, and increasingly more common, is to use a GPS receiver, taking a reading at the site and storing it in memory. The second method is to take two bearings with the compass on distant fixed objects which also appear on the map. The compass is laid on the map, and the position on which the lines from these two objects intersect indicates the find.

Mapping Scattered Remains

Human remains are frequently disturbed by a wide variety of wild and domestic animals. Species will vary with the geographic location, but certain general statements can be made. Large animals including bear, domestic, feral, and wild canids, and large wild cats will not only feed on surface remains, but will also disinter bodies from shallow graves. Smaller animals including rodents and ferrets will further scatter the remains. Corvids (crows and ravens), eagles, or vultures can deflesh remains and even carry small bones, teeth and dentures to their nests.

Cadaver dogs are an excellent means of recovering scattered remains. Dogs can be trained to find even small bones and flesh (e.g., digits). This can occur despite obscuring ground cover. Dogs can cover large areas in a fraction of the time that a human hands-and-knees search can be carried out. Their accuracy will also be greater in many instances.

Animal predation produces specific scatter patterns (see also Chapter 9). Understanding these patterns and properly mapping them can be of great assistance in solving a case. The original place of death or body disposition may not be the first place an alert occurs. It may be necessary to move both forward and backward to find the original site and to recover the maximum amount of material. Proper mapping helps ensure the best result.

When mapping scatter, one is working from the ground to create a map. Just as when reading a map to understand the ground, an appropriate datum or reference point must be established. The reference point may be the original body deposition site, the site of the first find, or an independently established point roughly perpendicular to the scatter path. The datum can be established on the ground by a GPS reading or by the intersection of two separate bearings.

Once the datum has been established, readings are taken to each discovered part. The reading must include both distance and angle. This can be accomplished manually with a tape measure and protrac-

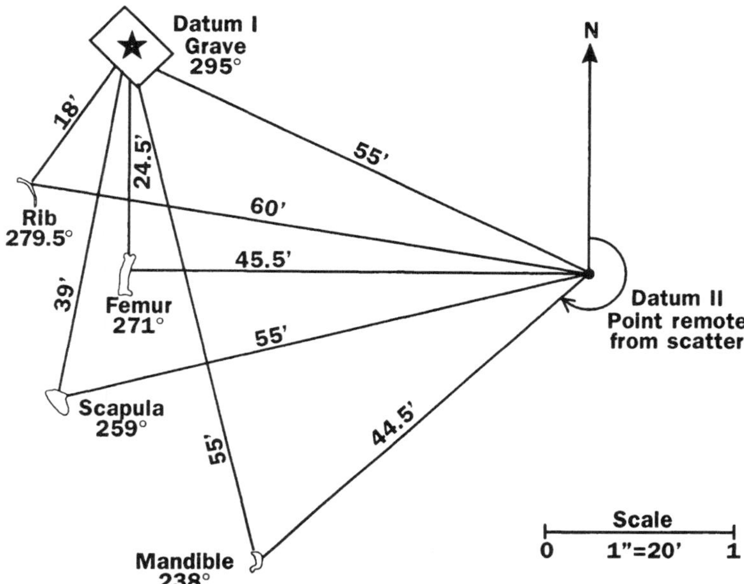

Figure 8.4 Mapping scattered remains. Construct a map triangulating scatter from two datum points. The angles are headings from north.

tor or with tools utilizing higher technology. The old-fashioned surveyor's transit has been replaced by laser-guided computer-integrated mapping technology. Unfortunately this technology is both expensive and difficult to deal with in the thick woods conditions accompanying many searches. An alternative is to use a hand-held laser range-finding system such as the Leica Disto and a sighting compass. These units are capable of an accuracy of 0.5 degrees.

Each reading is recorded and then a scale is set appropriate to the distances involved. The distances with the appropriate angles can then be translated onto paper creating a map. Alternatively, this information can be transferred to an already existing map. The actual scatter map is obtained by connecting the measured angles to points (see Figure 8.4).

USE OF REMOTE SENSING AND OTHER TECHNIQUES

Searches are frequently conducted with the help of a variety of techniques and equipment, often in addition to the cadaver dog team (see

France et al., 1998). Remote sensing equipment or other methods are used to locate promising areas that may not be visible or otherwise perceptible. There are also human observations used to infer the presence of the body.

HUMAN OBSERVATION

Human observation of subtle alterations in the landscape can often provide indirect evidence of a body's presence. Burials often leave telltale variation in the surface color, contour, and vegetation. Generally not all the fill dirt can be replaced within the hole and is left nearby. The surface over the body may become elevated (if a body is in the bloat decomposition stage) and later sunken (when the decomposition gases and soft tissue are lost). Depending on the length of time after death, vegetation over a buried body may be disturbed and removed (early on, due to the grave digging), then later may become relatively more lush than the plants nearby (due to the additional nutrients in the soil). Insect activity associated with a human corpse may be remarkably extensive, even if the body is buried in a relatively shallow grave. Swarms of flies rising from a decomposing body may attract visual attention during the early postmortem period.

SOIL PROBE

The dog's ability to pinpoint a buried body depends upon air exchange from below the soil surface. Certain soils, especially those with tight composition, may not allow much scent to reach the surface. Occasionally the handler will observe the dog working an area intently, but without being able to indicate an exact location. Another situation may arise with a burial on a slope, where the alert occurs at the bottom. In both of those situations, in order to locate the scent origin, the soil must be vented.

Soil in a suspected area can be vented with a soil probe, increasing air exchange and releasing additional scent. Changes in underground density (suggesting disturbed areas) may also be felt by the operator. These items (see Appendix A) can be purchased or made by a welder. The probe is inserted into the soil at regular intervals where the dog will be directed, or at an especially promising location.

The area to be vented should be well delineated. Start with one boundary and probe as deeply as possible approximately every 18 inches. After finishing line one, start a second line of holes offset from the first. Continue this technique until the entire area has been covered. As you proceed, you will become accustomed to the normal resistance in undisturbed soil. If using a core sampler probe, check initial samples from undisturbed areas to establish the normal types and depths of the various strata.

If you locate an area that has been disturbed, the probe will penetrate with less resistence. It is possible to determine the dimensions of the distrubed area with the probe. If using the core sampler, you will notice the strata are not defined, since the soil layers are intermixed when the area is refilled. You should then be able to locate the walls of the excavation. If a disturbed area, mound, or depression contains a body, you may detect decomposition odor on the soil that adheres when the probe is removed from the soil.

Use caution when probing a disturbed area! The probe can cause postmortem injury to the body or bones.

Once an area has been vented, let it rest a while—at least one-half hour—for scent to become available. This will clear the area of the scent of the workers and allow a more efficient search. Then work the dog in a tight grid, quartering the wind, to locate the area with the strongest scent. Check all disturbed areas carefully. Be careful not to "talk" your dog into a false alert.

OTHER METHODS FOR VENTING SOIL

We have used other, similar techniques for attempting to pinpoint a scent source, especially with older graves.

A post hole digger can be used easily in softer loam or sandy soils. Holes are spaced approximately two feet apart and a minimum of two feet deep. This method works well, especially if you are trying to locate a source on a hillside. In this situation, the dog will indicate on the holes below the source, but should give no reaction when searching above the source.

Trenches can be dug laterally on a hillside to attempt to find the source. They can be dug either with a shovel or backhoe. The depth is dictated by the type of soil and plant growth.

METAL DETECTOR

Metal detectors are used for both locating remains and recovering metallic evidence from a scene discovered previously. Although metal detectors may not be sensitive enough to detect projectiles lodged within a buried body, they may locate weapons, loose projectiles (bullets, casings) or items of body covering (belt buckles, shoes with metal parts). Such objects may be buried or may simply be obscured by fallen leaves or vegetation. Metal detectors are frequently employed during an excavation to assist in recovery of small metal objects that might not be caught in a soil screening process.

AERIAL PHOTOGRAPHY WITH AND WITHOUT THERMAL IMAGING

Aerial photography may be used to visually identify bodies or areas of soil disturbance. When combined with thermal imaging capability, areas that have a higher temperature may be identified, including decomposing bodies. These "hot spots" can be targeted for a more focused dog search.

OTHER TECHNIQUES

Ground penetrating radar (GPR), magnetic imaging (MAG), and electromagnetics (EM) are used. These techniques sense discontinuities in a substrate, such as a basement floor (cement or wood or dirt), or open ground outdoors. They create a printout that must be interpreted by an experienced technician. Areas that show up as disturbed (or in which discontinuous variation is detected) may be selected as possible locations of burials.

THE CRIME SCENE

The crime scene is a particular type of scene that requires specialized behaviors, attention to detail, and documentation. Although not all cadaver searches will end up being crime scenes, many will. And it is often not possible to know in advance whether a crime has been committed. For this reason, unlike the majority of search and rescue efforts, cadaver searches generally are conducted as if the site is a crime scene. This includes particular structures of scene command, site security and confidentiality, and documentation.

SCENE COMMAND

The person in charge will vary depending on the jurisdiction and the suspected events leading to the death. Sometimes the command structure will change if a body is discovered. For example, the search may be conducted under the direction of police, but once a body is found, the medical examiner may assume command of the recovery.

The cadaver dog team is part of a multidisciplinary forensic team whose members must cooperate and interact.

EVIDENCE PRESERVATION

Every dog handler must have a working knowledge of crime scene preservation and processing since the most innocuous lost person search may become a criminal investigation. Because a seemingly insignificant item may become a critical piece of physical evidence, the handler and dog must disturb the crime location as little as possible.

All dog handlers involved in a search are in a professional role, whether they are law enforcement officers or volunteers. Training in crime scene situations should be a part of every program. There are basic rules that every handler should know and follow under all circumstances, even if the situation appears perfectly innocent.

Any untimely or unattended death, regardless of cause, will normally be regarded as suspicious until otherwise determined by medical professionals. Even a death from natural causes, i.e., heart attack that is unwitnessed, will be the subject of an investigation.

The searcher who locates the victim must exercise caution to prevent the possible destruction of important physical evidence. Some examples of physical evidence include footprints, weapon, cigarette butts, matchbook, clothing, blood spatters, or items that might contain fingerprints. Not all evidence is obvious, so one must be cautious.

When you locate the victim, if the subject is obviously deceased, there is no need for you to disturb the body. (If you are uncertain, check for vital signs.) Contact the command post. If possible, remove your dog from the immediate area for his reward and prevent him from contact with the remains. This will prevent ball playing or other play reward from disturbing the ground around the body. If it is not possible, verbally praise the dog and place it on a down stay while you tend to the victim.

If the subject is alive, perform the immediate medical care necessary to stabilize the patient. If you must disturb any item at the scene, make sure to note where the item was originally. Inform the criminal investigator of any alterations.

If a weapon is visible upon approach, use caution. Do not touch or remove it unless absolutely necessary for your safety.

Do not allow other searchers to enter the area unless they are needed to assist with patient care. Make a record of anyone who is allowed access to the area.

There are three priority actions:

1. Secure the scene from disturbance
2. Cordon off the area for some distance around the scene (surveyor's tape can be used)
3. Do not allow anyone into the area without permission of scene commander or medical examiner

The cadaver dog handler finding human remains is responsible for maintaining the integrity of the scene until it is turned it over to a law enforcement officer or medical examiner. Once the handler relinquishes control, he or she should not reenter the area unless requested.

Note the overall picture of the scene. Draw a quick sketch map, showing the position of all items at the scene. Make notes of all your actions as soon as you turn the scene over to the authorities. Make sure you note to whom you relinquish control.

If you carry a camera, take some overall views of the scene from several different angles. But take care to avoid disturbing the area around the scene.

Write your report as soon as possible after the incident. Include all the pertinent details regarding when and where you were, why you were there, what you saw, and what action you took. Your report provides a written record for the investigation agency. You may use it to refresh your memory if you are later required to testify in court.

Remember the three cardinal rules to prevent scene disturbance:

1. Take the same path out that you took in
2. Do not add anything to the scene
3. Do not take anything from the scene

These procedures will minimize possible disturbance of the crime scene and allow the *chain of custody* for evidence to be preserved.

CHAPTER 9

BEHIND THE SCENES: TAPHONOMY

POSTMORTEM PROCESSES

Understanding the natural processes that influence outdoor death scenes is vital to the success of conducting and interpreting searches. The study of what archaeologists and paleontologists call "death assemblages" is termed *taphonomy*, which literally means the laws of burial, but can refer also to unburied bodies exposed on the earth's surface. In other words, taphonomy includes knowledge about the process by which a body is transformed from a living being to "dust"—or fossils, or chemical constituents, or mummified remains. Any of these postmortem processes, and the various paths they can take, may come to bear on what happens to a particular body after death. Only a very tiny percentage of bodies deposited in a natural setting will be preserved or become fossilized; most will decompose or be consumed by scavengers.

In archaeology or paleontology, scientists study taphonomic processes affecting the remains of organisms that died hundreds or even millions of years ago. But in *forensic taphonomy,* we are concerned with the earliest part of that postmortem period (Haglund and Sorg, 1997). More research is needed to understand these early transformations.

Every death, human or otherwise, has aspects that are unique and those that are generic. In other words, the circumstances and context of each organism's postmortem period are never exactly duplicated. And yet there are principles that tend to operate, creating general patterns that can be interpreted and occasionally even predicted.

DECOMPOSITION AND SKELETONIZATION

The breakdown of soft tissues and non-mineral components of bone occurs as a series of processes that begin at death. What was a dynamic, organized chemical system (the living organism) becomes less organized and more susceptible to outside influences. In many environments, the soft tissue ultimately liquifies and becomes separated from the bone. The mineral constituents of bone and teeth are much slower to decompose. Eventually, as soft tissue is lost, the skeleton may become completely exposed or ***skeletonized***. In freezing or very dry environments, soft tissue may not be lost and skeletonization may not occur or may be incomplete.

Temperature is the most important variable influencing the speed of decomposition. Chemical processes in living mammals are optimal near 37 degrees Celsius. Heating or cooling relative to that temperature will speed or slow the enzyme systems that control cell metabolism. At high temperatures (around 60 degrees Celsius) enzymes break down into their constituent amino acid chains and fragments (Gill-King, 1997). Freezing temperatures may halt most biochemical reactions.

If a body is placed in water, changes in temperature may be buffered and the pH may be altered. Depending on whether the water is salty, fresh, moving, or of a certain pH, the speed of decomposition in a submerged body may be faster or slower. Bodies in moister settings are more likely to give off scent because decomposition gases are water soluble. High levels of moisture also may encourage the formation of *adipocere* (also called grave-wax), as well as the growth of some plants and bacteria.

If bodies are in oxygen-deprived environments, such as in water, deeply buried, or at high altitude, decomposition may be slowed. Many bacteria are anaerobic, however, and low oxygen levels may actually stimulate their growth. In fact, *autolysis,* which occurs early on in cell death, results from lack of oxygen needed by enzymes. As a body goes through early autolysis, it also undergoes *rigor mortis*, with muscles stiffening, about 2–6 hours after death. At 4–6 hours it spreads to all the muscles, and remains in place for about 24–84 hours (Gill-King, 1997). In cooler temperatures, rigor occurs earlier and stays longer; warm temperatures can delay its onset or even keep it from developing completely.

At the end of the autolysis phase the system becomes very anaerobic. Bacteria in the large intestine and in surrounding soil grow rapidly, degrading the cells around them, and producing bloating, color change, and odor. This is the *putrefaction* and *fermentation* phase. Proteins are broken down to amino acids. The result of these processes is the presence of several toxic and volatile substances, including hydrogen sulfide, methane, *putrescine,* and *cadaverine*. The latter two produce the characteristic foul odor detectable by cadaver dogs (Gill-King, 1997). (These substances can be absorbed through unprotected skin and can compete with oxygen in respiration, requiring care on the part of recovery workers, particularly in closed and poorly ventilated settings.)

The bowel remains intact for some time as gases are produced, creating bloating. The bloating can cause a burial surface to rise, and can cause submerged bodies to float. In either of these cases, the temperature of the soil or surrounding water may be cold, delaying putrefaction. Bodies may remain submerged for several months of winter, rising to the surface only when spring warms the waters. If in very deep water, the body may never float.

Putrefaction causes dramatic color changes. Breakdown of hemaglobin produces the pigments biliverdin (which is green) and bilirubin (which is red) and subsequently urobilin (which is brown). Biliverdin in the skin may be converted to blue and yellow pigments. Hydrogen sulfide in the intestines can combine with iron to produce ferrous sulfite (black).

Adipocere, a waxy substance of varying consistency, may form within days or months given sufficient fats and moisture in the decomposition environment. Individuals who have a higher proportion of fat (such as obese individuals, more women than men, and infants) are more likely to produce adipocere. Not all bodies will produce it. In environments with more mineral content in soil or water, the adipocere is likely to be harder. It otherwise varies in texture from more crumbly to more paste-like.

The death of an organism sets in motion a complex array of natural processes that have evolved to recycle nutrients in the ecosystem. These include the actions of bacteria, fungi, carnivorous and omnivorous scavengers, insects, and even plants. The availability of these organisms, combined with the physical factors of temperature, moisture, oxygenation, and acidity constitutes the decomposition environment. This multi-factorial pattern is highly variable, making it difficult to generate rules about postmortem changes. Some general patterns can be expected, however:

- Temperature and humidity are the most important environmental determinants of decomposition speed.
- Protection from insect, bird, reptilian, and mammalian (and in the sea, crustacean or carnivorous fish) scavengers due to deep burial, body containers, or body covering will tend to prolong decomposition.
- Cold and freezing temperatures will slow or stop decomposition, while warm temperatures will speed it up.
- Lack of moisture enhances drying, hardening, and preservation of soft tissues.
- Traumatic injury tends to speed scavenger access and decomposition.
- Individual characteristics can speed decomposition: infants and children decompose faster than adults; smaller, lighter

individuals decompose faster; embalming and body covering slow decomposition.

- There will be a fairly large range of variation, even in the same geographic region.

Bass (1997); Mann, Bass, and Meadows (1990); and Rodriguez and Bass (1983) have studied the relationship between postmortem interval and condition of remains outdoors in the eastern mid-Atlantic region. They note that most soft tissue loss is due to maggots and other carrion insects, and that in hot, humid conditions a body can completely skeletonize in as little as 1–4 weeks.

Galloway et al. (1989); Galloway (1997); and Rhine and Dawson (1998) studied cases in the southwest and found that desiccation and mummification can be seen in as little as 2 weeks, whereas skeletonization can take up to a year.

Sorg, David and Rebmann (1997) report that non-scavenged remains outdoors in northern New England lose their skin, muscle, and ligaments (i.e., skeletonize) in 13–18 months, and their decomposition odor (to humans) between 13–18 months. Carnivore-modified remains are more variable.

DISARTICULATION

Disarticulation refers to the loss of contact between bones that normally form joints. This can be due simply to the loss of soft tissues, muscle, and ligaments that hold bones together. A body can become skeletonized and disarticulated, but the bones may stay in approximate anatomical position.

With the action of some taphonomic agents, such as large mammalian carnivores or water currents, the disarticulation can be more pronounced. Disarticulated bones may become scattered over fairly large distances, or they may be consumed and digested by animals.

Teeth may become separated from the jaws with the decomposition of the periodontal ligament that normally holds them in their sockets. They may then fall out due simply to gravity or due to movement of the jaw by animals.

SCAVENGER MODIFICATION

Understanding the manners and effects of animal scavenging on human remains is important in forensic contexts in order to locate scattered or partially consumed human remains or evidence. It is also important to discriminate scavenging damage from trauma due to the events of death, and to be able to estimate the time since death.

Levels of heat and moisture and access to scavenging insects, rodents, and carnivores are major agents of taphonomic change. For example, the patterned relationship between sarcosaphrophagous insects, such as flies and certain types of beetles, and decomposing bodies is fairly well known and used in forensic practice to estimate time since death (Haskell et al., 1997). Various "waves" of insect types will congregate and reproduce at different times during decomposition. Analysis of the types of insects present on a body and their metamorphic phases permits estimates of how long they have been there, particularly during the first couple of weeks, as well as the season of the death. Research using non-insect indicators to estimate time since death includes study of the condition of the remains, chemicals in the soil, plant roots and stems, and microscopic changes in the body.

Studying the behavior of scavangers also yields clues to taphonomic change. The scattering of bones by animals or water currents is apt to be patterned. Scavenging carnivores tend to be attracted when soft tissue is still present. As they pull on body parts, moving them away from the body for consumption or caching, bones may fall off along the way. The bones of the extremities (arms, legs, head) will likely be moved farthest.

More is known about canids (dogs, wolves, coyotes) and bears than other species. Research on the ability of cadaver dogs to locate decomposition scent even decades after death (France et al., 1992, 1996; Sorg, David and Rebmann, 1998) certainly suggests that scavenging behavior is a complex cluster of behaviors involving visual and olfactory cues, along with seasonal and species-specific consumptive patterns.

Haglund's (1997a) study of 33 cases with canid scavenging in the Northwest describes 5 levels of damage (see Table 9.1), associated with increasing times since death. With the cases in this study population, total disarticulation (stage 4) can occur in as little as 5 months. However, damage may be limited to stage 3 for as long as 11 months. It is important to note that the sample size is small and the range of variation is large. Further, these cases are illustrative of canids; other scavengers may have different patterns.

Sorg, David, and Rebmann's (1998) study of 36 outdoor recoveries in the Northeast, 21 of which were subjected to modification by large carnivores, also reports fairly large ranges of variation. Carnivore modification was more likely in deaths that occur in late spring (particularly involving bears) and summer, and less likely in deaths during autumn. Surprisingly, carnivore modification cases tended to have soft tissue for a longer period of time, possibly due either to small sample bias or to enhanced drying and hardening when elements are moved away from the moisture of the decomposing body. The condition of the remains was different on the extremities (which tended more often to be scattered and more weathered) than on the torso.

Table 9.1 Canid scavenging in the Northwest *(adapted from Haglund, 1998)*

Stage	Condition of remains	Time since death range in the study population
0	Soft tissue scavenging, no body unit removal	4 hours to 14 days
1	Destruction of abdomen and chest, removal of one or both arms and shoulders	22 days to 2.5 months
2	Partial or complete removal of lower extremities	2 months to 4.5 months
3	All skeletal elements disarticulated except segments of the vertebral column	2 months to 11 months
4	Complete disarticulation with only cranium and other assorted elements or fragments recovered	5 months to 52 months

Conclusions regarding scavenging and postmortem intervals can only be tentative. Scavenging of human remains, except that done by insects, is not well understood. Large animals appear to exhibit a few species-specific patterns. Bears are more apt to scavenge a body in the early spring when they emerge from hibernation, for example. But individual animals, circumstances, and environments create so much variation that interpretations concerning time of death based on scavenging patterns are only suggestive.

SEARCH STRATEGIES FOR DISARTICULATED REMAINS

Because of the importance of dental remains for doing identifications (Haglund, 1997b), special efforts should be made to recover teeth. Decomposition of the ligaments holding teeth in their sockets particularly affects single rooted teeth in the front of the mouth (incisors and canines), as well as all of the primary (deciduous) teeth. Furthermore, the skull (cranium and mandible) holds all the teeth and is easy for carnivores to carry away. Thus, every effort should be made to locate the cranium and lower jaw, as well as individual teeth that may have fallen out.

In order to maximize recovery, it is important to identify and map the dispersed elements as they are found. Sometimes teeth will be found imbedded in the soil beneath the spot where the cranium underwent decomposition. They may not be readily visible and this soil must be screened. In some cases the cranium may be moved, but a residual hair mass, clothing, or discolored soil may suggest the original location. Teeth may have fallen out before the cranium was moved; the search should be focused either at the hair mass or in the path between it and the cranium.

Sometimes the only indication of the original location will be decomposition scent, detectable only by the cadaver dog. Thus it is important that the handler note all alerts, even when no remains are seen at that spot. The remains may no longer be present, be too small to see, or have been incorporated into surface soil and debris. In some cases it is advisable to screen soil at an apparently blank alert site.

Strategies differ depending on the type of search requested. Sorg, David and Rebmann (1998) analyzed a series of 41 searches conducted by one experienced handler in the Northeast. About a third (29%) were recovery expansion searches, and 50% of these resulted in additional remains being located. Most (71%) were focused or unfocused speculative searches for individuals presumed dead. Of these, only about a third (29%) resulted in discovery of the body, and 64% are still missing. Thus, only 22% of the searches resulted in canine-discovered remains. The majority resulted in a no findings being made by the dog.

An analysis of all canine alerts from this series of 41 searches shows that the alert is a fairly reliable indication. Of the 45 alerts, 93% were associated with remains (either new discoveries or in areas where remains were found previously). This provides some confidence that the lack of an alert is also reliable. Komar (1999) reports the result of ten blind trials for eight teams; recovery rates averaged 81% with a range of 55% to 95% depending on the team. These results suggest that properly trained dogs can have a high success rate. Komar notes that recovery rates were depressed due to handlers' ignoring their dogs' alerts on decomposition fluid with no visible bone.

Haglund (1997b) suggests the following questions to guide the search in a recovery expansion or a speculative search in which remains are discovered:

- Are the remains scattered?
- From which original location were the remains scattered?
- What is the skeletal element composition of the scattered groupings of bones?
- What were the most likely trajectories of dispersion?
- Are there any special circumstances that might affect disassociation of teeth or scatter, such as explosive trauma?

Alternative strategies may have to be used if multiple scavengers are involved. Rodents or birds may carry teeth, small bones, dentures, or jewelry to their dens or nests. Teeth or bones may be consumed and expelled within animal scat (which must be searched; see Murad, 1997). Multiple coyotes or multiple bears may disperse remains in many directions. In these cases not only the presumed trajectory, but also the entire area, must be searched.

Because of the recent increase in the use of DNA for identification, it is important to treat every element as if it might become a DNA sample. This includes, for example, not touching any remains without wearing gloves. Otherwise, handler DNA may contaminate the bone.

WORKING WITH THE ANTHROPOLOGIST

Collaboration between the handler dog team and the anthropologist can increase the probability of success, particularly in scattered remains. The anthropologist trained in taphonomic patterns may assist in designing search strategies as the effort proceeds and remains are located. He or she will be able to identify individual bone elements or teeth for mapping, and an analysis of the distribution pattern may aid in making decisions about further searching.

CHAPTER 10

AT THE SCENE

INTRODUCTION

K-9 teams have been responsible for numerous technical assists to law enforcement agencies. Under actual field conditions, teams have located human remains buried for over 20 years, in graves exceeding four feet deep, as well as portions of dismembered bodies and/or disarticulated skeletal remains that have been missed by human grid searchers. Other accomplishments include locating many drowning victims, and pinpointing rape locations and homicide scenes where there was no visible physical evidence.

The tactics used for a cadaver search are similar to those employed searching for a live person in a wilderness setting. However, there are some differences. First, the amount of available scent may be quite small compared to that emitted by a live person, especially if the person has been dead many years. Second, if the remains are scattered there may be multiple scent cones, some with a very limited odor intensity due to their small size. Third, the body may be buried, resulting in a single scent cone in a more physically concentrated area. The handler must give careful attention to all of these issues, along with the potential size of the search area in planning the search in order to provide the maximum probability of detection.

GENERAL STEPS INVOLVED AT THE SCENE

- Assess the search type and potential size of the search area (survey versus detail, availability of other dogs, other searchers)
- Assess the terrain (on-lead, off-lead) and weather conditions
- Devise an initial search strategy
- Locate the scent cone(s). Is there be more than one? Is it pervasive?
- Direct the dog to find its source(s)
- Interpret possible scent cone distortions or interruptions
- Interpret the context of any alerts
- Interpret the context of the absence of alerts

ON-SITE GUIDELINES

Once the teams are on site, there are certain specific procedures that should be followed by scene commanders and by handlers to insure the most effective search effort:

DEFINE THE SEARCH AREA FOR THE HANDLER(S)

Keep personnel at the scene to a minimum. Provide necessary support services. When a properly trained cadaver dog team makes a find, they can initially secure the crime scene. The necessary investigators and forensic personnel can then be summoned.

If possible, allow experienced dog handlers to take the lead in setting up and running the search, in cooperation with scene investigators. They have the expertise to maximize the dogs' potential in conducting a proper, effective search.

If the search involves a large area, a minimum of two search teams should be used. When the search is for an old grave, results can be better evaluated if more than one team is used in the operation.

Do not establish an arbitrary time limit for the search. Psychological pressures caused by time constraints or excessive personnel can have an adverse effect on the search.

Do not expect miracles. Handlers should provide an honest opinion regarding the results. Many searches are initiated with only sketchy information from informants.

ACCLIMATING THE DOG

Once the search areas and strategies have been defined (see Chapters 11 and 12) and logistical support is in place, you are ready to commence your search. However, before you start, give your dog some time to get used to his surroundings, the people at the command post, and the general commotion. Let the dog relieve itself and make sure water is available. If you are working with other handlers, it may be a good idea to let the dogs meet the other dogs. If your dog has a tendency to be "dog aggressive," make sure you inform the other handlers and structure the search areas so that chances of a dog crossing into another dog's area are small.

MOTIVATING THE DOG

When you are ready to enter your assigned area, "fire up" the dog. Give the search cue in an excited manner. Some handlers like to set out a scent source and do a short search with an excited find to motivate the dog. Experienced dogs become highly motivated simply by the routine used to begin a search.

As you enter your area, let your dog do a free search while you assess the terrain. Walk through the area. The type and amount of underbrush and terrain features will determine your search pattern and grid width. If you have a large area, or an area with difficult terrain, you may want to walk the perimeter before you begin a directed search grid.

Watch your dog while you make your initial assessment. The dog may alert or may show heightened interest in one area. After you finish analyzing the area, you can begin your directed search. You may want to plan your coverage so that the dog is working where you have it in view as much of the time as possible, especially if the dog does a passive alert without doing a re-find.

Table 10.1 itemizes the various search patterns that can be used under differing circumstances. There will be times when you will use a combination of search patterns to cover your area. For example, if you are searching an area with a gully, you will probably use a combination of open (10-meter wide) and close (2-meter wide) grids using the terrain to establish your boundaries.

Initially your directed search pattern should quarter the wind to provide the best probability of detection for the dog. Concentrate on watching your dog. Don't let your observer or communications distract you. The initial indication may be subtle.

If you see an area where the dog appears to be interested, but there is no commitment, flag the area anyway. The dog may have gotten some odor on a thermal lift or simply be in an animal bedding area. If the dog appears to be working a scent pool, acknowledge it and give it time to see if it can locate the source. If no further interest is generated, continue on the initial search pattern. You can always research the area later. Adjust your pattern if there are significant changes in wind direction.

Watch the dog for signs of frustration or boredom. Rest and water the dog frequently. Follow the 20/10 rule. Twenty minutes of work, ten minutes of water, rest, or motivational play. Scent work is very intensive and the handler needs to be sensitive to the dog's needs.

If conditions are very warm, plan the search for cooler periods. Watch the dog carefully for signs of heat related problems. If working in hot, humid conditions, you may want to mix an electrolyte with the water.

If there is an area where the dog consistently shows interest, but in which you see no physical clues and the dog cannot seem to pinpoint for an alert, try to define the boundaries. Cross grid the area. If for some reason the dog still cannot pinpoint a source, flag the area and continue the search. Then approach the area of interest from a different direction. If the dog again shows interest but does not pinpoint, have another team work the area. If they get no reaction,

consider checking to see how well your dog is proofed against indicating human versus animal scent.

Be extremely cautious in taking the dog back to the same area several times in an attempt to pinpoint a scent source. The dog may decide that the odor it detects is the one it should indicate and give a false alert. A good rule of thumb is to work an area twice from two directions, then request that another team search it.

When all teams have finished their initial search assignments, and if no alerts have been reported, the handlers should swap areas and search as if the area had not been covered previously. The area receives double coverage and probability of detection is greatly increased.

PERIODIC REINFORCEMENT

You may want to make provisions for reinforcement, especially if you are involved in a large scale or multi-day operation. Close grid search, especially for buried remains, is an intense and difficult activity. Handlers, after working the dog for an extended period, may begin to wonder if the dog is really working. Watch the dog for signs of boredom or stress, and, if observed, take a break from the search temporarily.

A reinforcement problem can be set up outside the search area. It does not need to be difficult but should present some challenge. Completing a search with a find and proper reward from the handler should motivate and rekindle the dog's drive. The alert will also reassure the handler that the dog is working.

DOCUMENTING THE SEARCH

Chapter 5 provides a list of the components of a good search report. The details of the scene and the search effort are best recorded on site, during or just after the search. This will minimize inconsistencies and problems with memory.

Table 10.1 Types of Search Patterns

Pattern	Application
Free Search — Dog allowed to roam throughout area with no particular pattern.	Initial evaluation.
Open Grid — Dog works 25'-50' ahead of handler quartering the wind.	Relatively open areas. Wooded areas with light underbrush. Areas with good visibility of the dog by the handler.
Close Grid — Dog works within 5'-15' ahead of handler quartering the wind. Handler is able to observe the dog most of the time. Requires good control.	Dog can be directed into specific area, i.e., heavy brush. Gives higher probability of detection.
Cross Grid — Dog works a search pattern perpendicular to the previous search.	Increases probability of detection. Provides double coverage of area.
On-lead Search — Area worked with dog on long lead.	Heavy traffic areas. Residential area or inside building where distractions or dangers are present. Area where specific coverage is required.
Spiral Search — Dog is worked in a circle pattern from a specific point.	Used primarily in search for disarticulated remains.

CHAPTER 11

LAND SEARCHES

SEARCH PLANNING

Chapter 7 outlines the information needed to do good search planning. Once you obtain this basic information a decision can be made about how many teams are required to conduct the search. For example, if the search is for a recent victim, in a small area, based on information from a reliable informant, then one team should be sufficient. For the same search, however, if the victim disappeared 15 years ago, two teams should be sent. If the search area is large, or there are multiple probable areas, several teams may be required.

In most instances, it is a good policy to have a minimum of two teams respond if possible. In fact, a backup team is nearly always desirable. The second handler can act as an observer while the first team is working.

Before you leave for the search, work your dog on a reinforcement problem similar to the type of search you will be working. Attempt to duplicate the soil conditions and circumstances based upon the information you were provided.

CONDUCTING THE SEARCH

If multiple dog teams are assigned to the search, one handler should act as the search manager. He or she is responsible for assigning search areas, maintaining a master map of search activity, and generally supervising K-9 operations.

The dog handler(s) should make the decision on how the search is conducted (see also Chapter 10). When you arrive at the search scene, familiarize yourself with the projected search area. If it is a large area, obtain a topographical map. Define the boundaries and any outstanding landmarks. If a photographic aerial map is available, study it carefully for indications of old roads, logging trails, or open areas that might be accessible by vehicle. For search purposes, the photographic maps better reveal changes that can be referenced by the date of the survey.

The area should be divided into reasonable segments, using available landmarks to define each search area. If natural dividers are not readily discernible, then each boundary must be marked with survey tape.

If there have been previous search efforts, determine the type and the search boundaries. If the previous search teams have excavated, locate these areas. They will still be worked with a dog, but you will be aware of the cause of the recent soil disturbance.

Check the types of trees and bushes in the area. Trees with shallow, spreading root systems impede digging. If your search is for a grave, those areas become lower probability search sites. Dig a test hole with a shovel or entrenching tool to check the soil type and ease of digging.

The search manager should request that investigative personnel, if not selected to accompany a team, remain in a specific area. Investigators frequently expect the search team to make an immediate find. If they do not, they become bored and may begin their own foot search. Their wanderings may interfere with the dog team working a grid pattern. In reality, if an investigator is not performing a valid function at the command post, or in the field, he or she should not be at the scene.

Cadaver searches are normally conducted with support services nearby. The handler should not need to carry a lot of equipment. Each team should use a different color survey tape to identify search and alert areas. Probes, shovels, and associated equipment should be on hand. Water, compass, GPS, and maps should be carried by the handler.

A communications procedure should be set up. Use either your unit or the investigation agency radio frequency. If necessary, decide on a code word to use for when the victim is located. This is especially important if you are using a police frequency that is monitored by news media.

If possible, each search team should have an observer. Brief your observer as to what you expect from him or her, and how much space you need. Some handlers allow the observer to stay close, and others prefer they maintain a distance to the rear. Do not let conversation with the observer distract you from focusing on your dog!

You should be extremely clue-conscious during the search. Among the signs to watch for (see also Chapter 9) are:

- Unusual animal activity—Crows and buzzards are an indicator of carrion. Areas with animal digging may be an indication of buried carrion.
- Mounding or depressions—It is amazing how many of these occur naturally. However, with a burial there are likely to be other indications at the site, i.e., disturbed brush or residual soil. An

examination of the surface may reveal subsoil on the surface instead of humus.

- Differences in vegetation—Initially the surface vegetation will wilt. After a period of time, it may appear lusher than the surrounding plant life. There may be a color and/or height difference with the plants on the grave.
- Other unusual circumstances—The body or grave may be concealed by a brush or rock pile. Branches may be cut or broken, showing wilted ends. Anything that appears out of the ordinary should be thoroughly checked.

SPECIAL SEARCH SITUATIONS

There are some specific circumstances that require specific search tactics. These may occur at the outset or in the midst of doing a search. Most of the time a common sense approach will allow you to evaluate the situation and devise a reasonable plan to work the area.

SPOT SEARCHES

The spot search involves checking a number of locations such as lover's lanes, cul-de-sacs, gravel pits, etc., for remains. This technique is often used during investigations where only vague information is available.

Analyze each area for possible vehicle access. Check for any footpaths leaving the area and include them in your search plan. Make sure any refuse piles are checked.

Make sure you mark each area searched on your map, and note the date and time. The information can later be transferred to the master search map.

HASTY SEARCHES

A hasty, or non-thorough search (see Figure 11.1) is conducted to initially check an assigned search area, or in order to make decisions about search strategies. In this type of search, assumptions are made about the victim or perpetrator's behavior in order to identify higher probability areas. For example, the dog may be allowed to range freely around a natural perimeter or along likely paths. The hasty search is done to cover an area rapidly; it does not replace a logical and systematic grid search.

This approach is useful for very large expanses with no roads, particularly if there are only a small number of teams or a very limited time. It can be used to gather information about an unknown area or to narrow the search down to an area of higher probability. But, despite the hasty approach, these searches must be carefully mapped in

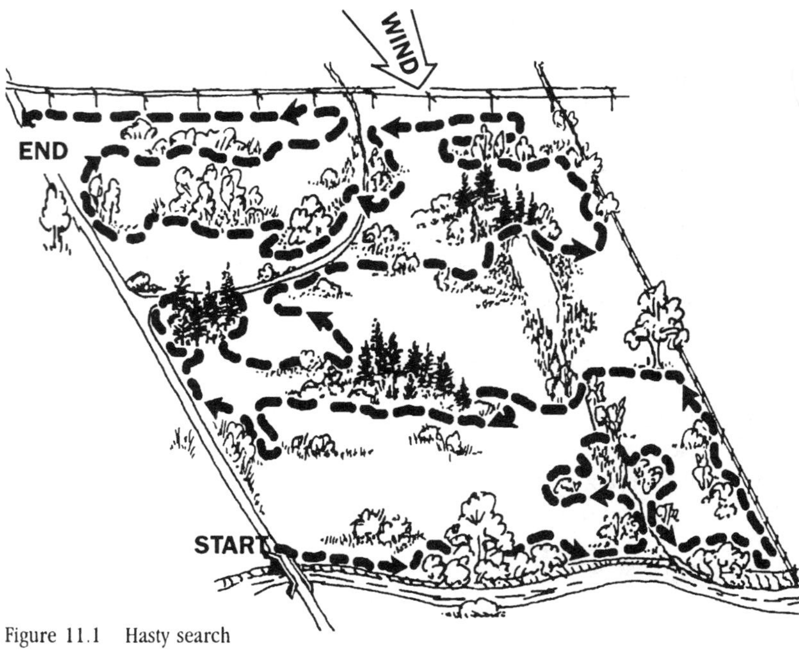

Figure 11.1 Hasty search

order to highlight holes in coverage that may need to be searched at a later time.

If looking for a subject who has health problems, or suffers from Alzheimer's, and if they have been missing for some time, the team may want to conduct a hasty search of possible paths of travel. In that case, work the dog along the path in one direction and, at the end of the sweep, move off the path on the downwind side and return to your starting point. Make sure the dog thoroughly checks all areas of heavy brush and any other obstacles where the subject may have hidden or taken shelter.

GRID SEARCHES

Grid searches (see Figure 11.2), also called thorough or corridor searches (discussed in Chapter 8 in the section on compass use), are the most systematic approach to investigating an area; they also take the most time. In this approach, passes are made back and forth through an area at regular intervals. Close grid searches utilize a very narrow corridor.

This type of search is appropriate with a flatter area that is relatively small and has no dense brush interrupting regular passage. It

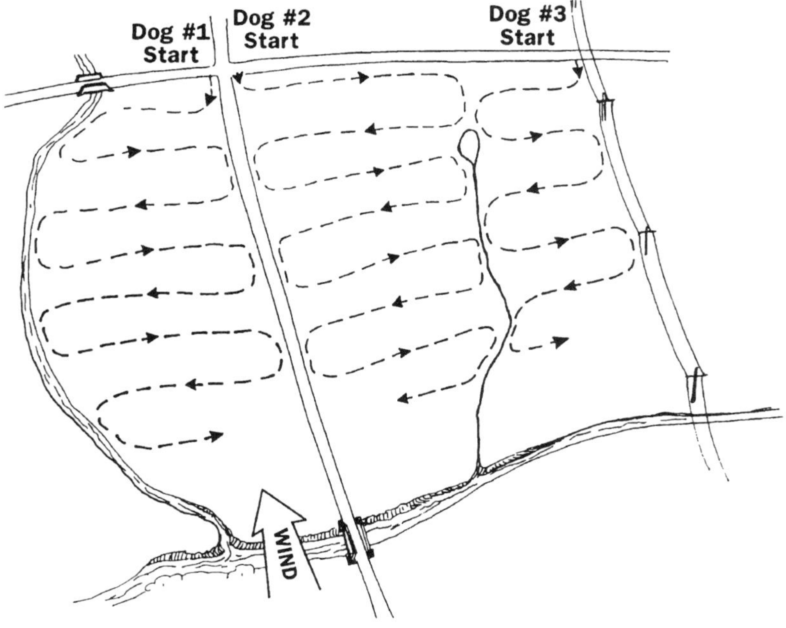

Figure 11.2 Grid or corridor search

also requires a relatively constant breeze. Grid searches are frequently used when there is more than one team and when a particular area has been identified for focus of resources and time. This sort of thorough coverage is useful with suspected burials for which scent cones may be reduced in intensity.

ROADSIDES

The roadside search occurs frequently and may cover a large lineal area. Since the area is shallow but long, the handler has to adapt his tactics to the situation. You probably will not be able to cross-grid the wind to optimize detection.

Analyze the terrain along the road. The investigators information may give an indication as to which side of the road is the most probable. There may be man-made (i.e., a deer fence) or natural barriers that would have restricted movement. The search pattern should extend at least 50 yards from the road. Be sure to include adjacent ditches or related footpaths. If the initial search is unsuccessful, then the far side of any man-made barrier would be a secondary search area.

Divide the area into manageable segments. One technique is to park your vehicle at the start of a segment, work a sweep for one-half mile from the vehicle, mark the end of the sweep, then make a second sweep on your return to your vehicle. For example, the first sweep might be made 10 yards inside the wood line, with the return sweep 30 yards from the road. If the dog is working 20-yard grids, then coverage would extend from the road to a depth of 40 yards.

Continue to work the road in segments until the complete distance is covered. Make sure all heavily brushed areas are well searched, since they are prime dumping grounds.

When searching steep embankments along the road, the first sweep should be along the top of the bank, since scent rises when warmed. The return sweep should be made at the base to detect scent that had pooled down slope. If the bank is heavily wooded, it may be necessary to make a sweep mid-slope, especially if you are working a high probability area.

LANDFILLS

Landfill areas pose special problems for the cadaver dog. The type and amount of organic matter decomposing under the dirt cover often provoke numerous alerts. Additionally, buried waste is not closely monitored, so there may be toxic chemicals present.

If you must search a landfill, attempt to have the dump operator identify the area where refuse was dumped during the time frame of the victim's disappearance. Daily records are usually required for this to be successful. Estimate the depth of the refuse, how tightly compacted the garbage is, and how much fill may be compacted over the refuse.

You can attempt to penetrate the fill with a probe, however, the chance of success is limited. Some common problems encountered include (1) the release of methane when a probe is used; (2) medical waste; and (3) large amounts of discarded foodstuffs. The operator of one landfill informed us that the area we were planning to search had at least 500 pounds of discarded meat from a supermarket.

By OSHA regulation, penetration over 4 feet deep must be handled as a "confined space search." This requires protective clothing, a breathing device, and decontamination upon search completion.

Posthole diggers can be used to drill into compacted refuse. Or, the landfill can be trenched with a bulldozer. Be cautious before entering any trench, especially if it extends into rotting garbage. The methane gas created by decomposition, among other substances, may be quite dangerous. Since the gas is heavier than air, it will remain in the bottom of the trench and you or the dog can be overcome. If you work holes made with a drill rig, alerts can occur because of the release of the common gases from decomposition of nonhuman remains.

Do not let your dog enter or drink any standing water, since it may be toxic. Make provisions for decontamination of the dog and handler after completing the search.

SWAMPS

Swampy areas can be difficult to search, especially if there is no access for a boat. By wading in a swamp, a dog's movements will cause the release of swamp gases, and may produce an alert. However, if the dog is allowed to acclimate to the pervasive gases, the area can be worked successfully. The dog will eliminate the pervasive odor and can concentrate on other scents.

If possible, work the area from a boat (see Chapter 12). The dog will be working scent on top of the water and not odors created by its own movement.

If a boat search is not feasible, attempt a search of the perimeter, watching for an alert to airborne scent. The alert may allow you to isolate an area for a more intensive search. Once you have an indication, you can grid your way into the swamp, watching carefully for a more intense alert and other visual clues.

WILDERNESS AND FOREST STRATEGIES

Most wilderness searches involve missing hunters, hikers, or people involved in specific activities (mushroom pickers, nature photographers, etc.). In order to develop a search strategy for such a missing subject, request information concerning their plans, familiarity with the area, physical fitness, and health. These subjects usually die due to an accident or pre-existing health problem. The search should be planned to cover the areas they may frequent.

Hunters: Game Trails and Stands

The search for a hunter will cover areas along the game trails or the area where he or she would normally establish a stand. Use an open grid pattern in a swath covering approximately 100 yards on each side of the trail. The subject may not be visible, especially if wearing camouflage clothing. If the dog gives any scent cone indication, it should be allowed to work it out, since the scent may be transmitted fairly long distances.

Hikers: Hiking Trails and Natural Hazards

The search for a hiker should cover both sides of the established hiking trail with special attention paid to areas that contain natural hazards. These might include cliffs (searched from the top and along the base, if possible), stream crossings (where the search will extend downstream for a distance commensurate with the depth and speed of water flow), and any side trails that they might have taken by mistake.

Other Lost Subjects: Open Grid and Large Area Search

Subjects other than hunters or hikers may wander through an area with no particular goal in mind. In these cases, the search becomes a large area search. Multiple dog teams should cover the area with an open grid, and any indication that the dog has hit a scent cone should followed up. This type of subject may be concealed in the undergrowth.

The best method to handle one of these searches is to develop a good search plan, make sure you cover the area well, working your grids on a compass bearing (see Chapter 8). Look for any physical clues that might have been left by the subject, and document their coverage.

DISARTICULATED REMAINS

When the subject has been missing for many months or years, it is likely the remains will be disarticulated and scattered. Searches are generally planned according to the guidelines above, depending on the type of victim. However, it is very important to use dogs trained to find multiple, small, and scattered remains. These scenes often include faint, overlapping scent cones. Dog response may be subtle. When victims have been missing many years, a closer grid may be required due to the loss of scent intensity.

Discovery by Pet Dogs

Many searches for disarticulated remains (recovery expansion search) are instituted after a human bone is brought home by a pet dog: typically, either the skull or a long bone. Attempt to ascertain from the pet owner the direction his dog normally travels, and the amount of time it is gone. Then you may be able to define probable search areas. In the majority of cases the site is within one-quarter mile from the residence. Even when bodies are extensively disarticulated, however, your dog will alert on the ground where the body initially decomposed. Frequently, there is also clothing and other evidence present.

Discovery by Hunters or Hikers

Another common recovery expansion search request occurs when a site has been discovered, but not all the body is present. Since the scattering has generally been done by scavengers, check for animal signs. You may be able to determine if the scatter is from domestic dogs, coyotes, foxes, bears, or other carrion based on the feces or prints. Feces may include bone or clothing; if so, it should be recovered. The anthropologist may be able to suggest an animal type based on the pattern of bone modification. Check for animal burrows and dens, or along game trails for additional remains.

Most remains are located within a 200-yard radius of the initial point. However, some cases in our database include scatter up to a mile.

DISMEMBERED BODIES

Dismemberments are either the result of an accident, such as an airplane crash, or a deliberate attempt to conceal the body of a homicide victim. Portions of the bodies of accident victims may be spread over a very large area of land or water, whereas deliberate dismemberments tend to be more localized.

Accidental Dismemberment

If an aircraft explodes in flight, the search areas for human remains can be plotted by mapping the areas where debris lands. If the accident is caused by impact, the search will encompass a smaller area. Generally an attempt will be made to locate all the remains before the debris is removed. These pieces may be quite small. The extreme fragmentation and dispersal due to a crash may literally bathe the scene in scent and produce initial confusion for the dog. A close grid search is generally required (in order to locate all the small fragments), and adequate time is needed for the dog to acclimate to very subtle differences in scent distribution.

Deliberate Dismemberment

The dismemberment of a homicide victim may occur for several reasons. The first is to remove hands, head and possible means of identification. The second is to make handling of the body easier. In the first instance, the portions of the body may be discarded or buried in separate areas and some portions may never be located.

In the second instance, the remains are normally buried in the same grave or in several small graves in the same geographical area. Thus, the dog may alert in several locations even though there is only one victim. If the dismembered corpse was left above ground, animals will probably have scattered it.

A classic dismemberment case was the Connecticut "Wood Chipper" homicide. Portions of the victim's body were processed through a commercial wood chipper and the chips were discarded along a rural road. A trained dog alerted to wood chips located next to the road in a drainage ditch. Even after extensive scene processing, the only parts recovered were a tooth, fingernail, and flesh totaling three ounces. The torso, or other body parts were never located. Nevertheless, the evidence recovered was sufficient to result in murder conviction.

A search for portions of human bodies will, of course, produce multiple alerts from the dog. The dog should be reinforced for each find. The dog naturally will attempt to re-find the located remains, so the handler will have to direct it to continue the search.

SCENT LINE-UPS

A K-9 cadaver search team may be asked to perform a scent line-up, or may be asked to search a focused area (such as a vehicle or group of vehicles) to attempt to locate possible forensic evidence, or determine if a body had been in a particular spot. The results may be considered for use in a trial or as the basis to obtain a search warrant for that vehicle or specific premises.

If the dog alerts, there may not be any visible evidence since the dog may be detecting residual scent. This refers to a residue of scent that remains detectable for some time. Generally this is due to small amounts of decomposition chemicals that have sloughed off of a body.

Line-up identification may be used to locate an item with residual decomposition scent. For investigative purposes this may involve, for example, several articles of clothing or several vehicles. The goal is to see if there is or has been a body in a specific location, or if the clothing, weapon, or other artifact might have been in contact with the body, blood, or decomposition fluids. Based on the actions of the trained dog and the conclusions of the handler, the investigator can apply for a search warrant.

The line-up must be conducted "blind" and under controlled conditions. In order for the results to be credible to a judge, the handler can instruct the investigator in how to structure the situation, but must have no knowledge of where the item actually is placed. If it is a vehicle line-up, the handler should not possess any information about the suspect vehicle.

The dog must perform its full, trained indication or alert when the article is located in order for the results to be acceptable and believable to the judge. The handler should take precautions to insure the results are not tainted, that is, to avoid the possibility the dog was cued to alert on an item. If the dog is worked on a loose lead or off lead, the dog can initially indicate the presence of the target odor by a body language change and then perform its trained alert.

Procedure for Scent Line-ups

The procedure to set up the scent line-up includes the following steps:

1. The dog and handler should have been trained previously to work a line-up.
2. Prior to the procedure, the handler should describe to the investigators the indication his or her dog is trained to give.
3. All items or vehicles are put in place without the handler present. Careful instructions should be given to personnel setting up the line-up.
4. Items to be tested are generally spaced 6–8 feet apart. This spacing

allows the dog to make up its mind and prevents scent overlap to adjacent items.

5. Items or vehicles should be numbered. For a vehicle line-up, similar types of vehicles should be used. A court will not consider a line-up that includes marked (or unmarked) police vehicles and one civilian vehicle, for example. If an item or clothing array is to be examined, the items may be placed in paper evidence bags that are numbered and open at the top.
6. If the line-up consists of an item or clothing array, the negative items should be put in place first to minimize the possibility of cross contamination. Disposable gloves should be worn by personnel handling the items. Care must be taken not to touch a negative item with the gloves worn handling the target item.
7. Only one dog team should work the line-up at a time. If several teams are available, the team that has trained and proven most reliable in training should be selected. If practical, the dog should be off lead. The dog may be worked on lead, but the handler must maintain a steady pace, allow the dog to work out in front, and should be careful not to cue the dog to any specific article.
8. If off lead, the dog should be allowed to work the line-up at its own speed. The handler must generally control the dog, making sure it checks each item, and does not just randomly wander around the area.
9. If an item containing the target scent is present, the dog must perform its full, trained indication.
10. The line-up should be diagrammed showing the relative positions of the items used.
11. The line-up should be videotaped. The court may allow the tape to be shown at trial.
12. There should be at least two impartial witnesses, preferably from the law enforcement agency or the prosecutor's office.
13. A document of the search should be made by the handler, as for any search, and a record kept on file.

ADAPTING TO SPECIAL TERRAIN AND SITE CIRCUMSTANCES

Because the conduction of scent is dependent upon the wind in combination with the terrain, it is important to take both into consideration when devising search strategies. Natural terrain features can be used to divide the area for multiple teams (see Figure 11.3) or for a single team. For example, old railroad grades, paths, waterways, and ridges provide natural boundaries and access. Using any feature that aids mapping and navigation will speed the search process. When there

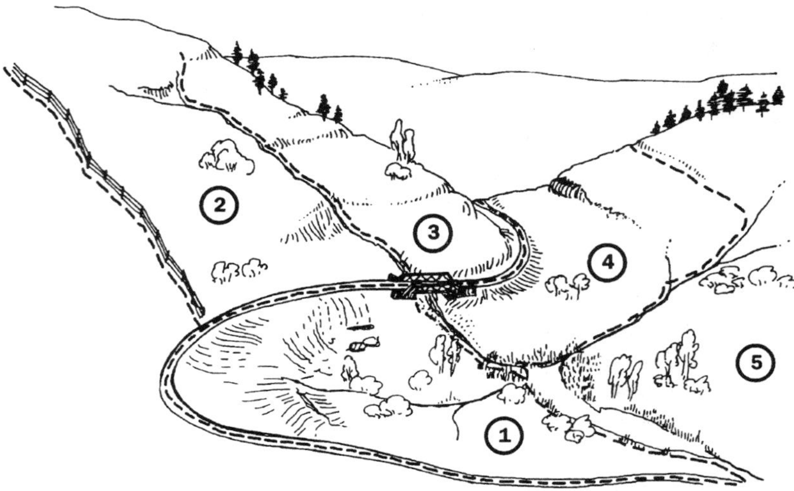

Figure 11.3 Dividing a search area for multiple dog/handler teams.

are undefined boundaries, one method to avoid flagging them first is to have two teams work toward that boundary and "bounce" off of each other.

CHANGES IN ELEVATION

Try to start the search on a higher point, giving good visibility and access to scent rising upslope (updrafts) as the heat of the day increases the surface temperature (see Figure 11.4a). There will be downdrafts going down a hill's slope in evening and night as the land surface cools (see Figure 11.b). If searching in very early morning, there is an increased probability of picking up scent from higher elevations; if searching during midday, there is better probability of detecting scent from lower elevations. The prevailing wind may act to reduce or accentuate the effects of updrafts and downdrafts, depending on its direction.

CONTOUR SEARCHING

When the terrain is hilly, it is advantageous (wind direction permitting) to move along hill contours rather than using more energy going up and downslope (see Figure 11.5).

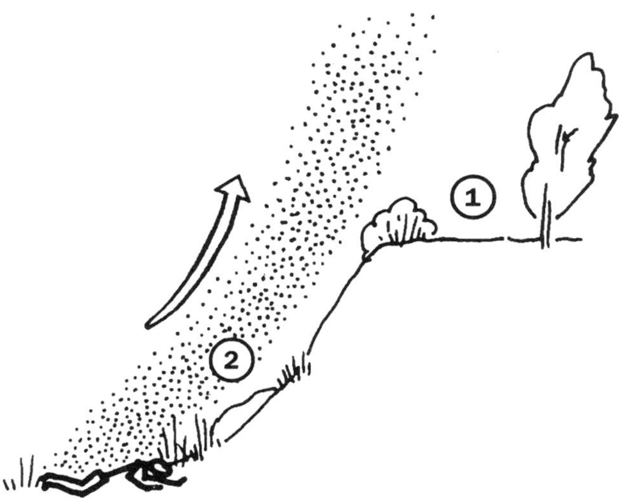

Figure 11.4a Updraft creating scent void (1), and remote scent cone (2) above the body.

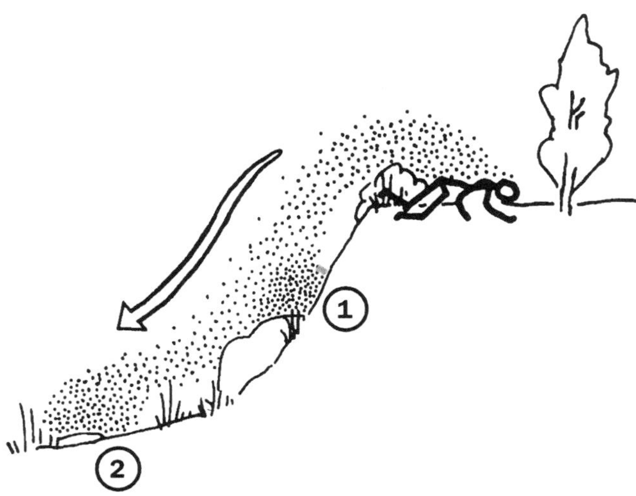

Figure 11.4b Downdraft creating remote scent pools below the body.

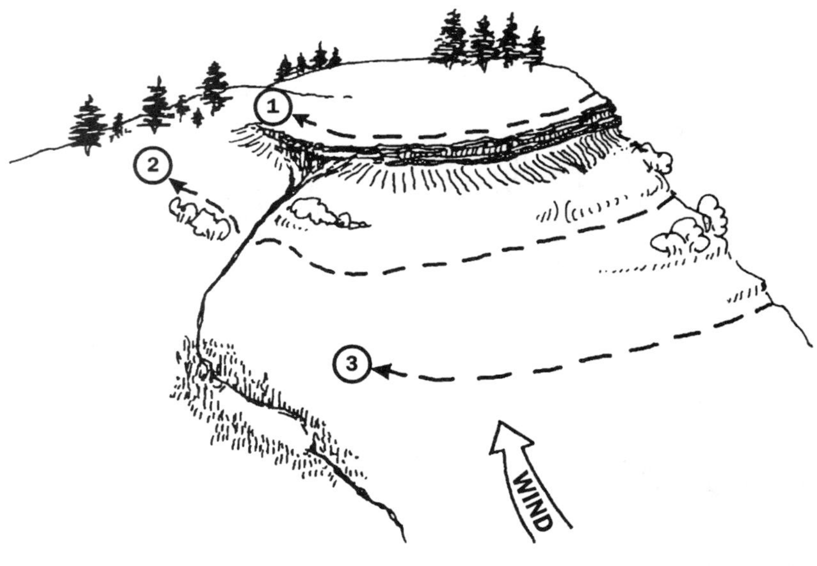

Figure 11.5 Contour search

DRAINAGE PATTERNS

Keep in mind that waterway drainage paths (and road cuts) may cause the wind (or drafts) to funnel and concentrate within them. Attempt to maximize time spent moving perpendicular to the wind. If the wind is moving in the wrong direction and you cannot change your path, use smaller corridors.

If a watershed is being searched thoroughly, it is helpful to begin at the higher elevation and make contour passes back and forth across the stream (assuming it is not too deep). This maximizes time spent moving downhill, rather than going parallel to the stream and having to move uphill with every other pass (see Figure 11.6a and b). If doing a hasty search of the same area, the best access is probably downhill along the stream regardless of wind direction.

WELLS

Wells present a special set of circumstances. Remains in wells may be relatively protected and hidden, underwater and inaccessible to scavengers. The scent is not likely to rise up the shaft. It may be necessary to search for where the underground waterway that feeds the well finally reaches the surface, downstream from the well. Or a sample of well water can be provided for the dog to smell.

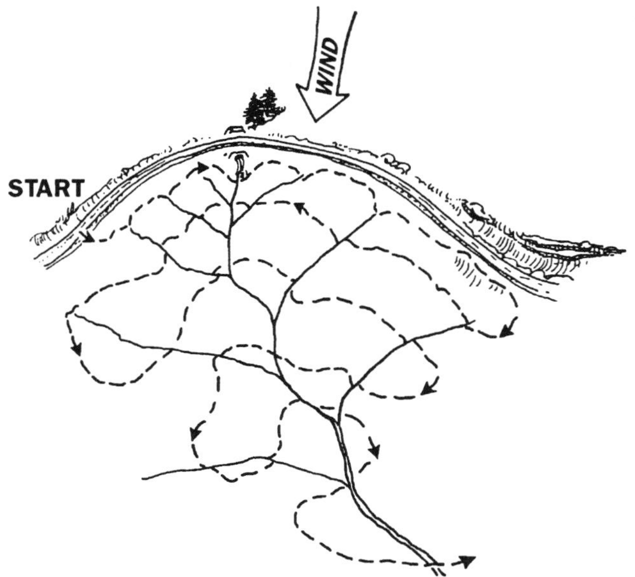

Figure 11.6a Thorough search of a drainage

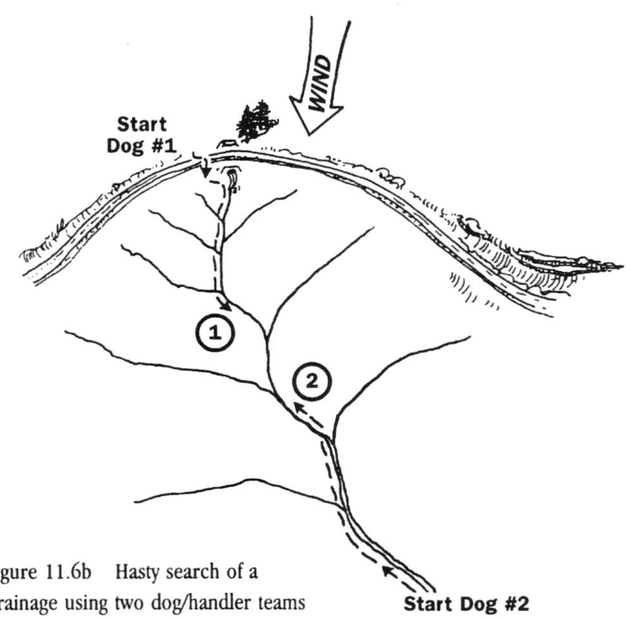

Figure 11.6b Hasty search of a drainage using two dog/handler teams

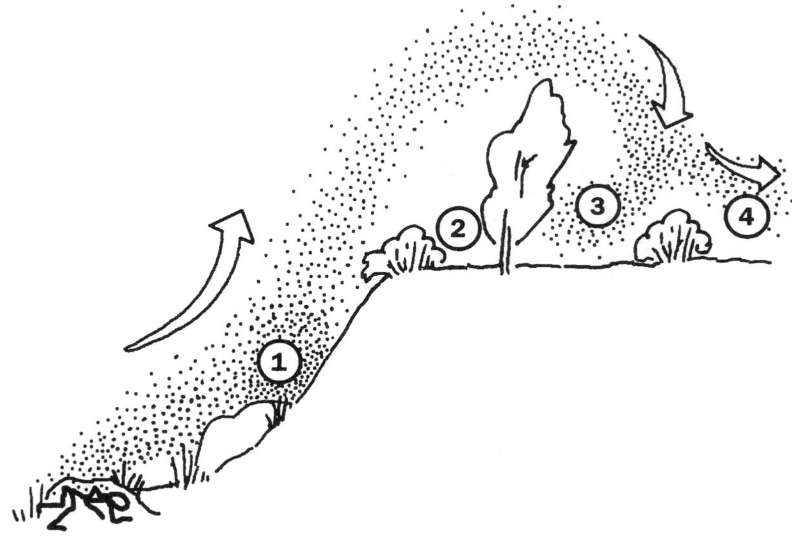

Figure 11.7 Interpreting complex alerts. 1 & 3: remote scent pools; 2: scent void; 4: remote scent cone

DIFFICULT TO EXPLAIN ALERTS

Occasionally the dog's alert may be difficult to interpret. Complex combinations of change in terrain and vegetation, air movement due to temperature variation, and obstacles can all create scent pools and scent voids remote from the body. Figure 11.7 illustrates the creation of several scent pools and voids formed as the scent rises up slope from the body, pools behind a rock, flows over the top of the tree and pools behind it, and continues to form a secondary scent cone on the far side of the bush. Consider alternative explanations for scent origin that takes into account these factors.

CHAPTER 12

WATER SEARCHES

By Marcia Koenig

Dogs have been used to find bodies under water since the mid-1970s. Andy Rebmann has documented searches from this time where his trailing bloodhounds followed subjects' scents to bodies of water. Through a change in body language, each dog indicated the trail ended there. Based on the actions of the dogs, divers searched and found the subjects in the water. *Water searches* are now a normal aspect of cadaver dog searches. This chapter covers specific training techniques and materials. It also reviews search strategies particular to water locations.

TRAINING

The water search training program is designed to let dogs know that subjects can be found underwater, observe the dog's natural alerts, and to shape a strong, trained alert. As is true for general training, the dog's behavior must be shaped in small increments so the dog has a chance to succeed, be rewarded, and do many repetitions.

TRAINING MATERIALS

See Appendix A for sources, addresses, and contact numbers.

Sigma Chemical Company has developed a *scent capsule* that simulates the scent of a drowned person: Sigma Pseudo™ Drowned. It is relatively inexpensive and easy to use. A trainer can train by himself or herself using the chemical. Dogs trained exclusively with this chemical have had no difficulty finding subjects on actual searches.

Another training aid is a *scent pump* (see Figure 4.1c). The scent material is put in a tube. Air is pumped through this tube into the water using compressed air or a hand bicycle pump. The simplest and easiest to use scent pump is assembled by Multi-SAR Technologies and marketed by Search Gear. Using the scent pump requires two people: one to run the pump and one to train the dog.

Divers simulating the victim are the most fun and rewarding for the dog and handler. Even though the diver is alive and not drowned, the dog gets the idea that humans can be found underwater. However, using divers requires a lot of coordination, time and people involved. Divers are best used when the dog already has learned the concept of the water search.

TRAINING STEPS USING A SCENT CAPSULE

1. Choose an area along a shoreline that is long enough so the dog can walk along it without having to go directly to the scent source. The water should be shallow and slow-moving.
2. Prepare the scent source. A *scent cage* (see Figure 4.1b) can be used in the initial stages to give the dog something to target. Put a line on the scent cage so it can be retrieved from the water. Put a scent capsule in the scent cage and toss it in shallow water.
3. The capsule will last from 10 to 45 minutes depending on water temperature. If the capsule dissolves too quickly in warm water, put it in a pill or film container with holes punched in it. You can put hair in the container to further slow the rate of dissolution.
4. Walk the dog on lead along the shore. Start downstream from where the scent cage was tossed in.
5. As soon as the dog looks in the direction of the scent cage, praise the dog (or use the clicker) and pull the cage out of the water. Then give the reward.
6. Encourage the dog to touch, sniff, or play with the cage.
7. Do the same problem two or three times more. You are looking for recognition by the dog that human scent can be coming from under the water. The cage gives the dog something to focus on. Don't forget to reward your dog every time.
8. When the dog realizes that scent is coming from under the water, add the *trained alert*. The dog will do a *natural alert* without being trained. Learn to recognize your dog's body language. On water searches this could be an increasing interest in the water, biting at the water (the dog has scent glands in the roof of the mouth), staring at the water and scratching and whining leading to barking. In contrast, the *trained alert* is what the dog is trained to do to tell the handler it has found the scent of the subject. This could be a bark, a *down*, getting a toy from the handler—a specific behavior that tells the handler the subject is under the water at that location. It might be one of the natural alerts, just stronger. The dog needs to make a definite commitment to the scent source.
9. Set up the problem the same way as before and work it several times in several sessions prompting the dog to give the trained alert.
10. Vary the training sessions by varying where you place the scent

source: in shallow water; in deeper water; next to the shore; farther out (be sure the wind blows to where the dog can pick it up); from a dock; from a boat.

11. When working from a boat, suspend the scent cage from a bobber. Add weights until the bobber floats just under the surface. This prevents the dog from cueing on the bobber. If you have problems with the dog alerting on bobbers and buoys, put several out, only one of which has the scent source suspended under it. If the dog alerts on the wrong buoy, say no in a neutral voice and encourage it to search for the correct buoy.
12. When the dog gives the trained alert five times in a row, without prompting, you are ready to do a blind search. Remember that any skill takes many repetitions.
13. Do a *blind search*. Have a helper flick the capsule into the water along the shore (no scent cage) so that you do not know where it is. Work the dog down the shore watching for the natural alerts and then the trained alert. Let the dog work the problem and make up its own mind. If the dog is having problems, have the helper tell you where the capsule is, and then assist the dog in working it out.
14. When the dog is successful working a blind problem from the shore, do a blind problem from a boat. Unless the water is shallow (10 feet or less), have the helper suspend the capsule from a bobber. If the capsule is too deep, there may not be enough scent for the dog to alert. Proceed as in #13.

TRAINING USING A SCENT PUMP

The scent pump is very good for intermediate and advanced work. For use with beginners, put the air stone in a scent cage. Training is easier if the dog has something concrete to focus on.

TRAINING USING A DIVER

Dogs can be trained for water search using capsules only, scent pump only, diver only, or a combination of the three. If it is difficult to schedule divers, save them for advanced training. A diver is a fantastic motivator for the dog. If all training prior to this has been done with capsules and scent pumps, nothing excites the dog like a diver surfacing with its toy.

There are two potential difficulties working with divers. Signaling is the first problem. Work out a signal system so the diver will surface when the dog alerts. The most successful is a two-way radio system. If the diver does not have radio communications, beat on the side of the boat with a metal pole, use an air horn, or attach a line to the diver (with diver's permission). The second problem is bubbles. Some dogs may cue on the bubbles. Ways around this are to work when the water is little choppy or to put a couple of air tanks in the water, only one of which has the diver attached to it.

Safety for the diver is the first concern. Let the divers decide how long they can work and under what conditions. Plan the training session so things go smoothly and quickly. If you are training more than one dog, have two boats so one can be going out with a handler and dog, while the other is returning with another handler and dog.

See Appendix A for reference to a video showing training progression using divers.

BACKGROUND INFORMATION—TYPES OF DROWNING

DRY DROWNING

Dry drowning occurs in as many as 15% of drownings. These are not actual drownings, but are deaths from traumatic causes, such as a blow to the head or entry into frigid water (activating the mammalian dive reflex, which excludes water from the lungs). In such cases, there is no (or minimal) fluid in the lungs. This type of victim is likely to float downstream on the surface with the current before finally sinking. A child will float even better than an adult.

WET DROWNING

In a *wet drowning* the victim will have fluid in the lungs. As water closes over the victim's face, the oxygen supply is cut off. The victim stops struggling, loses consciousness and gives up the residual air in the lungs, aspirating water. The body goes down near the point last seen. It will stay at the bottom until enough gasses build up in the body cavities to return it to the surface. Then it will start floating downstream as it rises. For example, a jumper off a bridge will usually be found within a few feet of where he or she entered the water, even if the person was struggling and river current was strong, as long as the search is done within a few hours.

SEARCH STRATEGY TIP

If possible, determine the type of drowning, dry (trauma) or wet. If dry, expect the body to float with the current. If wet, start looking for the body where it was last seen.

EYEWITNESS

An eyewitness can give you the point last seen and might be able to tell you if the victim was hit by an object (dry drowning). If it is a wet drowning, the victim will be in the immediate area indicated by the observer. This can be difficult to pinpoint from the bank of a river or lake with just one eyewitness, but it is a place to start. With more than one witness you might be able to triangulate to the place last seen.

Without an eyewitness, empty boat, or debris, you do not know where to start. It becomes an unfocused speculative search, and the potential search area is greatly increased.

SEARCH EXAMPLE

A family was out all day at the river. When it was time to go home the father and four children walked in the river to avoid the muddy banks. At one point all four children slipped. The father grabbed the two youngest and got them up on shore. He saw one of the remaining children bobbing under a bridge but never saw the other one. The child seen bobbing under the bridge was found floating 1/4 mile downstream an hour later. He had slipped and hit his head (dry drowning). Dogs alerted on the second child in an 18-foot hole in the riverbed close to the point last seen (wet drowning). He was never recovered because divers had removed a large tree near the point last seen, causing the current to change course and adding nine feet of silt in the hole.

DECOMPOSITION PROCESS

FIRST STAGE

A short time after death microorganisms start producing gas inside the body. The rate of gas buildup depends on the temperature of the water. Depth does not make a substantial difference in the usual lakes and rivers; it is temperature that controls the speed of gas buildup. However, in deep water (100'-200') pressure reduces the volume of gas, so more gas has to be produced to create buoyancy. Decomposition also is faster if the stomach is full.

SECOND STAGE

During the second stage the body will bloat to buoyancy and float to the surface (so long as it does not get hung up on debris or buried). This depends on the temperature of the water surrounding the body. This process can take 24-72 hours if the water is warm, and months if the water is cold.

THIRD STAGE

When the body surfaces, it may float until recovered, or it may disintegrate and sink, never rising again.

EXCEPTIONS

If the temperature of the water surrounding the body is too low for bacterial action, i.e., under 37 degrees Farenheit (Carpenter, personal communication), the body may never decay enough to float up to the surface. Deep lakes often have thermal layers that do not permit warmed surface water to mix with the water at the bottom and so the body will likely not surface.

If the body is not intact, for example, the chest or stomach is open, it will not bloat and rise to the surface.

WORKING A WATER SEARCH

SELECTION OF BOATS

The type of boat chosen for the water search can make the search easier or more difficult. But, the dog handler often must use whatever is available. If there is a choice, the following factors make some boats better for scent work than others.

Height Above Water

Use a boat that is as low to the water as possible. There is more scent at the surface of the water. Dogs often "taste" the water for scent, and some like to swim in it to get the scent of the subject. *Caution: only allow the dog to swim if you work in calm water. It is too dangerous to permit your dog to swim in whitewater rivers.*

Motor Type

The boat should move as slowly as possible. An electric trolling motor is excellent and does not produce fumes. A gasoline engine can work if care is taken to keep the fumes downwind of the dog and it is run at as slow a speed as possible.

Oars are good on a lake, particularly to decrease the "hot" area where the dog is indicating.

BOAT TYPES

The best place for the dog to pick up the scent is in the bow of the boat, particularly if he has room to move around. Height above the water is the most important factor. If you can purchase a boat, the following are the best choices

1. Inflatable Zodiac-type boats. These are the best all-around boats to use for water search. The boat can be transported easily, and the dog can get very close to the water. Make sure it has a hard floor; otherwise, the dog will have difficulty walking around.
2. John-boats. These are one of the best boats for moving slowly. They are particularly good in shallow water.
3. Bass and trolling boats. These are also good for water work as their

sides are low to the water. They usually have electric motors and run very slowly.

4. V-hull boats. These boats are not quite as good for water search as the bow tends to be out of the water more. They do have an advantage of being large enough so there is plenty of room for the dog to walk around the deck and to work both sides of the bow.

WORKING A SEARCH AREA

GENERAL SUGGESTIONS

1. Give the dog the opportunity to scent the people in the boat.
2. Watch for people on the shore. If possible, try not to have spectators on the shore downwind of the dog. If you cannot do anything about it, give the dog a chance to get used to the spectators. Then focus the dog's nose down to the surface of the waters.
3. Do not work the area when divers are in the water; the dog will alert on the divers.
4. Place a trained dog handler on the shore as an observer. The observer can often see faint alerts that the handler misses because of his perspective. If several dogs work the area and alert, the observer at a distance is better able to discern the "hottest" area.
5. Use a second dog to work the area without telling the handler the area of the first dog's alert. It is always good to have a second dog confirm (or not) the first dog's alert.
6. Mark the alert area with a buoy. Do this after all dogs have worked the area. Some dogs will cue on any article in the water.
7. When the air temperature is near freezing or below, the rate of evaporation is low, and scent may not rise very far above the surface of the water. The dog may have to be almost on the surface of the water to catch the scent.

SUGGESTIONS FOR WORKING RIVERS

If possible, grid the area systematically back and forth from bank to bank. Have another person direct the gridding so the handler can pay attention to the dog. A river channels the wind up or down its length. So, there are four ways to work a river problem (see Figures 12.1 and 12.2):

- upstream against the wind
- upstream with the wind
- downstream against the wind
- downstream with the wind

The most desirable situation would be to work upstream to the point last seen with the wind coming toward you. However, that is not always possible. If it is a whitewater river, downstream may be the

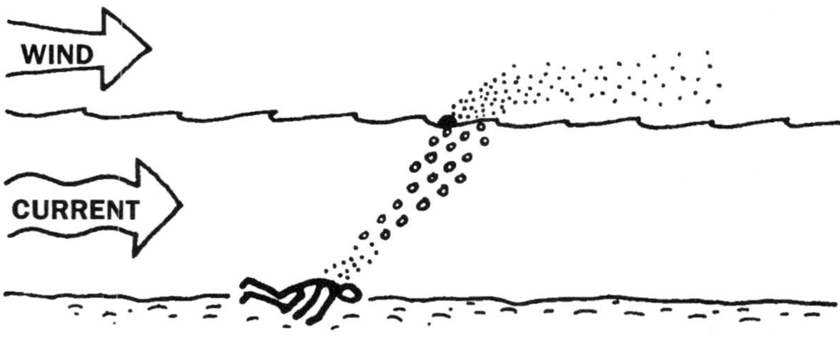

a. Cross-section view

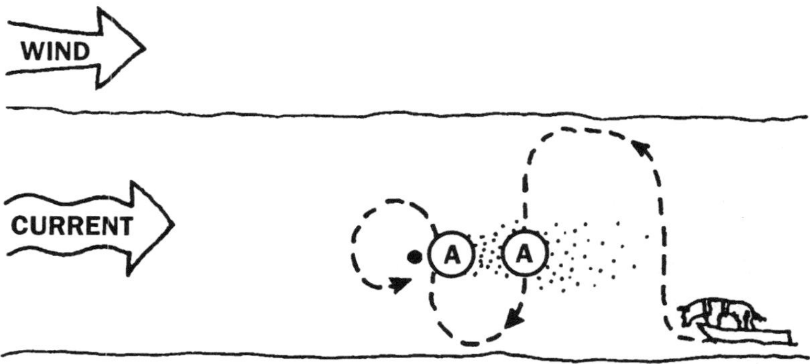

b. Searching against wind and current—overhead view

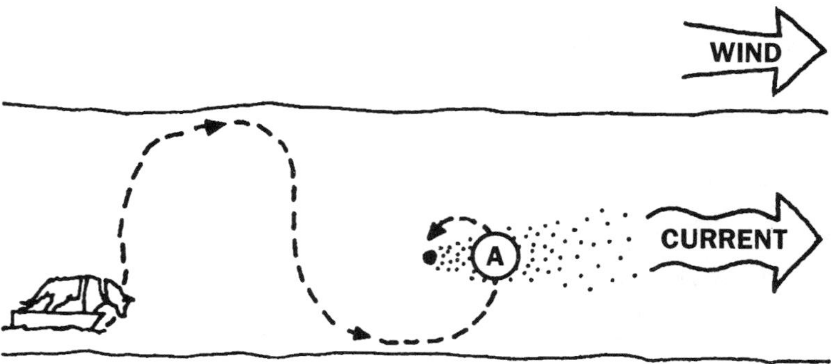

c. Searching with the wind and current—overhead view

Figure 12.1 Wind and current in same direction. A = location of alert.

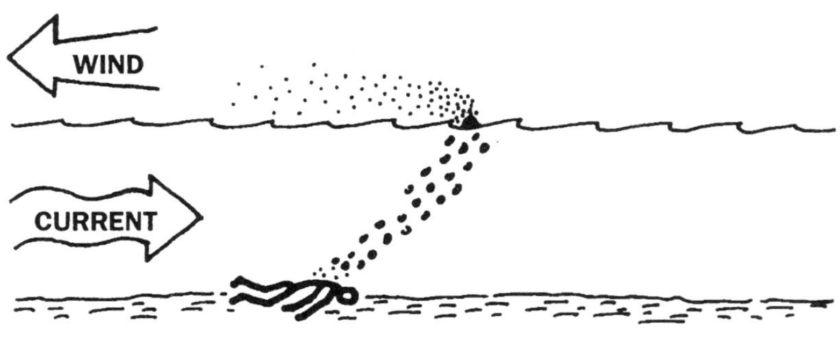

a. Cross-section view

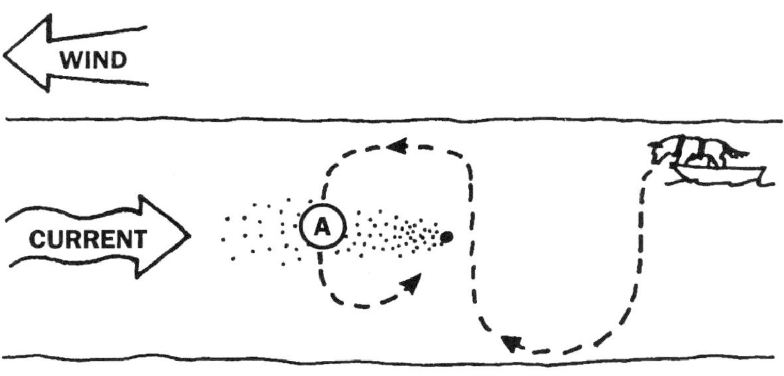

b. Searching withwind and against the current—overhead view

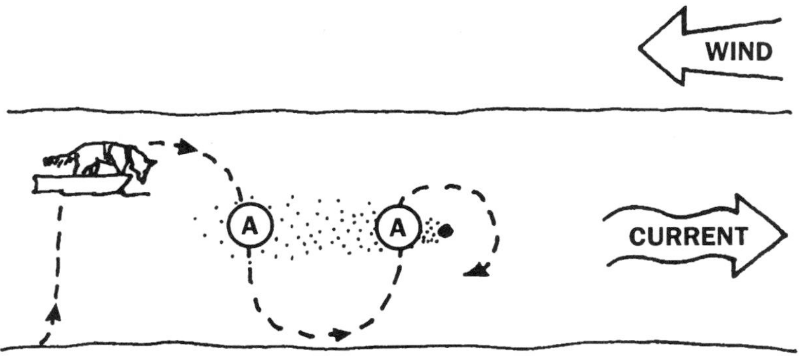

c. Searching against the wind and with the current—overhead view

Figure 12.2 Wind and current in opposite directions. A = location of alert.

only way to search it. Following are suggestions for how to work rivers upstream and downstream and the types of alerts to be expected depending on wind conditions.

Upstream Against the Wind

Work into the search area below the last known point, if possible, going across from bank to bank. That gives the dog time to work the problem out and the handler time to see the transition from "no alert" to "alert."This is the same as working an air scenting problem on land. The handler and dog work upstream, the dog alerts until he loses the scent. The point where he loses the scent is the point where you pass the body (see Figures 12.1a and 12.1b).

Upstream With the Wind

Work the problem the same as upstream against the wind. The difference here would be the alert. Because the wind is carrying the scent away from the dog, he will not alert until in the vicinity of the body. The alert will come all suddenly instead of gradually (see Figures 12.2a and 12.2b).

Downstream Against the Wind

Start above the last known point. The scent cone is coming toward you so the dog will alert, move into the scent, and then lose it when he passes over the victim's location. This, also, is similar to an air scenting problem on land (see Figures 12.2a and 12.2c).

Downstream With the Wind

Work the problem the same as downstream against the wind. Again, the difference is the length of the alert and where it is strongest. As the dog passes over the victim's location, he will alert suddenly. Then the alert will get weaker as he moves out of the scent cone (see Figures 12.1a and 12.1c).

SUGGESTIONS FOR WORKING LAKES

On a lake, work into the wind if possible. With a small lake, the handler can cut the area into sectors. If there are no alerts in a sector, it can be eliminated. That way a small area can be cleared systematically. This grid pattern can be run on a compass course, with a GPS, or by lining up landmarks. Have a second person, who also knows about dogs, direct the grid pattern. This is in addition to the driver of the boat. That way the handler can give the dog undivided attention.

WATER CONDITIONS

A wet drowning victim usually just sinks under normal conditions. But under flood conditions or where there is turbulence from a dam or in whitewater, the body might not sink. The force of the water can wash it away from the point last seen. River eddies and strainers are good places to check because they trap and contain debris.

RECOVERY

The biggest problem for dog handlers is that they usually do not see the recovery. An alert by the dog and possible location of the body by divers may take only a short time. The body recovery may take several more hours or even days depending on water conditions.

Dive recovery is a difficult three-dimensional problem for the divers. Conditions may be so demanding on the bottom (current, murky water, submerged trees, etc.) that the divers are unable to work the area systematically and may just miss the body. So if the body is not found by divers, it does not mean it is not there. Dogs can help the divers know where to look, but no water search is worth risking the loss of a diver. Follow up after a water search to see if the body has been located and where. Feedback will give you information to improve your skills.

If the water is too dangerous for divers to work, the agency may elect to wait for the body to surface. The agency may decide not to use dogs to pinpoint where the body is submerged as they will not be able to recover it from that location.

"FALSE" ALERTS

In a water search, the victim is usually hidden and not accessible. This means that the handler must rely on the dog's actions for information. Alerts are clues. A "false" alert is the dog cueing in on something other than the victim. It may be on clothes, dead wet critters, submerged debris catching and holding scent, a marker buoy, or the handler's body language.

MARKER BUOYS

The dog should not alert on objects in the water. This can be corrected by telling the dog to "leave it" in a neutral voice, and by placing three or four buoys in the water and ignoring any alerts on the buoys.

CLOTHING AND OTHER DEBRIS

In training, ignore alerts on clothing. You want the dog to look for the strongest source of scent: the victim.

DEAD, WET CRITTERS

It has been thought that dogs will also alert on dead, wet critters. However, Debra Tirmenstein, Missoula County, Montana Search and Rescue, has researched this question through observations and tests set up on road-killed animals. She found that "...the more training a dog receives, particularly in exposure to cadaver search techniques and in scent discrimination drills, the less likely false alerts on animals or on other potentially 'confusing' odors, such as decaying vegetation, sewage, and swamp gasses, etc., will be" (Tirmenstein, 1998, p.238). Set up problems where the dogs will encounter dead animals and human odors (divers, Pseudo™ Drowned capsule, or scent machine). Reward alerts on human odors, and ignore interest or alerts on animals. If necessary, tell the dog to "leave it" in a neutral tone of voice.

HANDLER CUEING THE DOG

This is one of the biggest problems handlers have. For example, the dog may be showing mild interest in something in the water. The handler sees the dog's interest, thinks it might be an alert on the victim, and through words or body language cues the dog to increase its intensity. The handler may unconsciously be prompting the dog in his or her eagerness to get a strong positive alert. But the handler does not know what the dog is alerting on, or if the dog is alerting at all. In a training situation, you encourage the dog. In an actual search situation, let the dog do the work and make up its own mind. Be quiet and do not cue the dog! If it has had training on hidden subjects (snow, rubble, water, etc.), the dog should make the "decision" about where the scent is strongest. The handler's job is first to observe and then to reward the dog after the dog alerts.

Water searches need to be interspersed with training sessions. That gives the dog the opportunity to earn jackpots, keeping his interest up. It gives the handler the opportunity to train the dog and observe him under controlled conditions. Observe on practices and observe on searches. Videotape the exercises and searches and go over them yourself and with others. The more you observe yours and others' dogs, the easier all search problems will become.

Acknowledgments

Portions of this chapter are based on conversations with Andrew Rebmann; Tish Taber and Vern Dombrowsky, Search Dogs, Inc., MN; Marian Hardy, Mid-Atlantic D.O.G.S., MD; Kathy and Rich Fifer, Cascade Dogs, WA; Debra Tirmenstein, Western Montana Search Dogs; and personal observations.

BIBLIOGRAPHY

BOOKS AND ARTICLES

Bass, W.M.
1997 Outdoor decomposition rates in Tennessee. In W.D. Haglund and M.H. Sorg (eds.) *Forensic Taphonomy*. Boca Raton, FL: CRC Press, pp. 181-186.

Becker, R.F. and J.E. King
1957 Delineation of the nasal air streams in the living dog. *Archives of Otolaryngology*, 65:428-436.

Bryson, S.
1996 *Police Dog Tactics*. New York, NY: McGraw-Hill.

France, D.L., T.J. Griffin, J.G. Swanburn, J.W. Lindemann, G.C. Davenport, V. Trammell, C.T. Travis, B. Kondratieff, A. Nelson, K. Castellano, and D. Hopkins
1992 A multidisciplinary approach to the detection of clandestine graves. *J. Forensic Sciences*, 37:1445-8.

France, D.L., J.J. Griffin, J.G. Swanburn, J.W. Lindemann, G.C. Davenport, V. Trammell, C.T. Travis, B. Kondratieff, A. Nelson, K. Castellano, D. Hopkins, and T. Adair
1997 Necrosearch revisited: Further multidisciplinary approaches to the detection of clandestine graves. In W.D. Haglund and M.H. Sorg (eds.) *Forensic Taphonomy*. Boca Raton, FL: CRC Press, pp. 497-510.

Galloway, A.
1997 The process of decomposition: A model from the Arizona-Sonoran Desert. In W.D. Haglund and M.H. Sorg (eds.) *Forensic Taphonomy*. Boca Raton, FL: CRC Press, pp.139-150.

Galloway, A., W.H. Birkby, A.M. Jones, T.E. Henry, and B.O. Parks
1989 Decay rates of human remains in an arid environment. *J. Forensic Sciences*, 34:607-616.

Gill-King, H.

1997 Chemical and ultrastructural aspects of decomposition. In W.D. Haglund and M.H. Sorg (eds.) *Forensic Taphonomy*. Boca Raton, FL: CRC Press, pp. 93-108.

Haglund, W.D.

1997a Dogs and coyotes: Postmortem involvement with human remains. In W.D. Haglund and M.H. Sorg (eds.) *Forensic Taphonomy*. Boca Raton, FL: CRC Press, pp. 367-382.

1997b Scattered skeletal human remains: Search strategy considerations for locating missing teeth. In W.D. Haglund and M.H. Sorg (eds.) *Forensic Taphonomy*. Boca Raton, FL: CRC Press, pp.383-394.

Haglund W.D. and M.H. Sorg (eds.)

1997 *Forensic Taphonomy*. Boca Raton, FL: CRC Press.

Hancock, E.

1996 A primer on smell. *Johns Hopkins Magazine,* 47(4):21-22, 25.

Haskell N.H., R.D. Hall, V.J. Cervenka, and M.A. Clark

1997 On the body: Insects' life stage presence, their postmortem artifacts. In W.D. Haglund and M.H. Sorg (eds.) *Forensic Taphonomy.* Boca Raton, FL: CRC Press, pp. 415-448.

Hodgson, M.

1997 *Compass & Map Navigator: The Complete Guide to Staying Found.* Merrillvill, IN: ICS Books, Inc.

Katz, S.R. and C.R. Midkiff

1998 Unconfirmed canine accelerant detection: A reliability issue in court. *J. Forensic Sciences,* 43(2):329-333.

Komar, D.

1999 The use of cadaver dogs in locating scattered, scavenged human remains: Preliminary field test results. *J. Forensic Sciences,* 44(2):405-408.

LaFave, W.R.

1996 *Search and Seizure: A Treatise on the Fourth Amendment,* 3rd Edition. St. Paul, MN, West Publishing Co.

Letham, L.

1995 *GPS Made Easy: Using Global Positioning Systems in the Outdoors*. Seattle, WA: The Moutaineers.

Mann, R.W., W.M. Bass, and L. Meadows
1999 Time since death and decomposition of the human body: Variables and observation in case and experimental field studies. *J. Forensic Sciences,* 35:103-111.

Morse, D., J.Duncan, and J.Stoutamire (eds.).
1983 *Handbook of Forensic Archaeology and Anthropology.* Florida State University, Tallahassee, FL: Rose Printing Co. (available from Jack Duncan, 3705 Longchamp Circle, Tallahassee, FL 32308).

Murad, T.A.
1997 The utilization of faunal evidence in the recovery of human remains. In W.D. Haglund and M.H. Sorg (eds.) *Forensic Taphonomy.* Boca Raton, FL: CRC Press, pp. 395-404.

Pryor, K.
1999 *Getting Started: Clicker Training for Dogs.* Waltham, MA: Sunshine Books, Inc., pp. 3-12. (Also appeared in *Dogs In Canada Annual,* 1992.)
1999 *Don't Shoot the Dog: The New Art of Teaching and Training.* New York, NY: Bantam Books.

Rebmann, A.J.
1993 Cadaver dog training using pseudo scents. *NASAR Conference Proceedings.*
1994 *Cadaver dogs: A primary resource for the location of human remains.* Unpublished manuscript, Redmond, WA.

Rhine, S. and J.E. Dawson
1997 Estimation of time since death in the southwestern United States. In K. Reichs (ed.) *Forensic Osteology: Advances in the Identification of Human Remains,* 2nd Edition. Springfield, MO: C.C. Thomas, pp. 145-160.

Rodriguez, W.C. and W.M. Bass
1993 Decomposition of buried bodies and methods that may aid in their location. *J. Forensic Sciences,* 30:836-852.

Sachs, J.S.
1993 The fake smell of death. *Discover: The World of Science,* 17(3):87-94.

Simpson, B.S.
1997 Canine comunication. *Veterinary Clinics of North America: Small Animal Practice,* 27(3):445-464.

Sorg, M.H., E. David, and A.J. Rebmann
1997 Cadaver dogs, taphonomy, and postmortem interval in the Northeast. In K. Reichs (ed.) *Forensic Osteology: Advances in the Identification of Human Remains,* 2nd Edition. Springfield, MO: C.C.Thomas, pp. 120-144.

Steen, J.B., I . Mohus, T. Kvesetberg, and L. Walloe
1996 Olfaction in bird dogs during hunting. *Acta Physiol. Scand.,* 157(1):115 (abstract).

Stoddart, D.M. (ed.)
1980 *Olfaction in Mammals.* London, UK: Academic Press.

Syrotuck, W.
1972 *Scent and the Scenting Dog.* Mechanicsburg, PA: Barkleigh Productions, Inc.

Tirmenstein, D.A.
1997 Scent discrimination in canine water Ssarch. *National Association for Search and Rescue, Conference Papers,* May 27-30, Portland, OR, pp. 231-247.

Thesen, A., J.B. Steen, and K.B. Doving
1993 Behaviour of dogs during olfactory tracking. *Journal of Experimental Biology,* 180:247 (abstract).

Tolhurst, B.
1991 *The Police Textbook for Dog Handlers.* Sanborn, NY: Sharp Printing.

Tolhurst, B. and L. Reed
1984 *Manhunters! Hounds of the Big T.* Puyallup, WA: Hound Dog Press.

VIDEOTAPES AND OTHER REFERENCES

Koenig, M.
1989 *Water Searching with Dogs.* K-9 Specialty Search Associates. (videotape)

Carpenter, B.
n.d. Research by Johnson County, Iowa, Sheriff, personal communication.

APPENDIX A

RESOURCES

SELECTED TRAINING AIDS AND EQUIPMENT

AERIAL PHOTOGRAPHY OF THE U.S.

Terraserver
http://www.terraserver.com

CADAVERINE AND PUTRESCINE

The chemical substances cadaverine and putrescine can be obtained from a commercial chemical supplier, but are not recommended because of the difficulty in handling and the precautions that must be observed when working with the substances.

COMPASSES

Brunton Company
620 East Monroe Avenue
Riverton, WY 82501
(800) 443-4871
http://www.brunton.com

Silva
Johnson Worldwide Associates
1326 Willow Road
Sturtevant, WI 53177
(607) 779-2264
http://www.silvacompass.com

GLOBAL POSITIONING SYSTEMS (GPS)

Magellan Systems
960 Overland Court
San Dimas, CA 91773
(909) 394-5000

GPS World
P.O. Box 7677
Riverton, NJ 08077-7677
(800) 237-4582
http://www.gpsworld.com

MAPS AND MAPPING SOFTWARE

Delorme Mapping Company
P.O. Box 298
Freeport, ME 04032
(800) 452-5931
http://www.delorme.com

Maptech
655 Portsmouth Avenue
Greenland, NY 03840
(800) 627-7236
http://www.maptech.com

The Map Store
98 N. Main Street
Old Town, ME 04461
(207) 827-4511

Topozone
http://www.topozone.com

United States Geological Survey (U.S.G.S.)
(800) 872-6277

NATURAL HUMAN DECOMPOSITION SCENT

You may be able to obtain other training materials through the medical examiner or coroner. These may include clothing or other items. If you plan to use flesh or bone, research your local and state laws to make sure that you are in compliance. Certain states prohibit the collection and use of human remains for canine training.

OTHER INFORMATION SOURCES

Karen Pryor
Sunshine Books, Inc.
49 River Street, Suite 3
Waltham, MA 02472
(800) 47 CLICK; FAX (781) 389 0754
http://www.clickertraining.com http://www.clickerpet.com

PSEUDO™ CORPSE FORMULATION I & II AND PSEUDO™ DROWNED VICTIM

Product Number	Product	Purpose
P4304	Pseudo™ Corpse Formulation I	For early detection (0–30 days)
P3929	Pseudo™ Corpse Formulation II	For post-putrefaction detection
PSC-1	Corpse Scent Kit	Contains two applications each of Formulation I and Formulation II
P7184	Drowned Victim Scent Formulation	Used in training for water search

Product may be ordered from:

Sigma Chemical Company
P.O. Box 14508
St. Louis, MO 63178
(800) 325-3010
http://www.sigma-aldrich.com

SOIL PROBES, FLAGGING, AND DISPOSABLE GLOVES

Types of soil probes include

- Solid (3- to 4-foot length, 1/2- to 5/8-inch diameter). Suitable for all types of soils. Easy to fabricate using 1/2-inch bar stock with one end sharpened to a point. The handle should be 12 inches in length and may be covered with plastic tubing for operator comfort.
- Core sampler (3-foot length). Difficult to use in rocky soils. Allows examination of strata for evidence of soil disturbance.
- Tile probe (42- to 60-inch length, 3/8-inch diameter). Has a ball welded to the end of the probe. Easier to use in tight soils.

Ben Meadows Company
P.O. Box 80549
Atlanta, GA 31366
(800) 628-2068
http://www.benmeadows.com

SCENT TUBES, WATER SCENT GENERATOR, AND GENERAL SEARCH SUPPLIES

Search Gear
882 Bruce Lane
Chico, CA
(800) 474-2612
http://searchgear.com

Scent Cage Container for scent to be used in training for water searches is a cricket cage used commonly by fishermen.

Soil Samples Can be dug at the site that a body decomposed. You may be able to obtain permission from the law enforcement agency to obtain soil once the crime scene has been processed and released. If the body decomposed in a wet area, adipocere may be present for collection. Make sure that you take proper protective measures when obtaining the samples and store them properly.

Weather Meter, Pocket

Neilsen Kellerman
104 W. 15th Street
Chester, PA 19013
(610) 447-1555
http://www.kestrel-instruments.com

CONTINUING EDUCATION OPPORTUNITIES

TRAINING

K-9 Specialty Search Associates

P. O. Box 5100
Kent, WA 98064-5100
(253) 630-0444
http://www.cadaverdog.com

Offers the following classes:

Basic Cadaver Search Seminar (3 days, 24 class hours) The seminar is designed to give search dog handlers a working knowledge of cadaver search. It covers training principles and methods and allows time for hands-on training.

Water Search Seminar (3 days, 24 class hours) This is an intensive seminar to prepare handlers for water search for the drowned victim. It combines classroom instruction with intensive hands-on water work. The emphasis is on developing reliable, readable alert and proper search techniques to conduct a water search successfully.

Basic K-9 Cadaver Search (7 days, 56 course hours) This intensive training program is designed to prepare K-9 handlers to conduct an effective search for human remains. It combines classroom instruction and practical field work in aboveground and buried body search techniques and an introduction to water search for drowned victims.

Advanced Cadaver Search (5 days, 40 course hours) Prerequisite: completion of the Basic K-9 Cadaver Search course. This class concentrates on search planning and management, realistic search problems, evidence and crime scene search, disarticulated remains, and residual scent work. The class sets up, manages, and documents a speculative search.

PROFESSIONAL ORGANIZATIONS

NATIONAL ASSOCIATION FOR SEARCH AND RESCUE
4500 Southgate Place, Suite 100
Chantilly, VA 20151-1714
http://www.nasar.org

NORTH AMERICAN POLICE WORK DOG ASSOCIATION
4222 Manchester Avenue
Perry, OH 44081
http://www.napwda.com

NORTH AMERICAN SEARCH DOG NETWORK
P. O. Box 508
Patterson, TX 77466-0508
http://www.nasdn.org

APPENDIX B

REPORT EXAMPLES

K-9 SEARCH REPORT

Requesting Agency:	Florida Department of Law Enforcement Special Agent Ray Dyal Pensacola Field Office Pensacola, FL 32513 (904) 444-8570
Victim:	JANE DOE Victim disappeared from the Big Bad Wolf Convenience Food Store, Route 15 and Red Wolf Drive between 2330 and 2400 hours on February 18, 1991.
Date of Search:	January 28 to 31, 1995
Location of Search:	Four locations in Santa Rosa County, Florida
Type Search:	K-9 used to search areas for possible buried human remains.
K-9 Teams:	Andrew Rebmann with *Marianne*, a six-year-old German Shepherd search/cadaver dog. Dog operational since 1988. Nancy Jones, Northwest Florida Search & Rescue Assn. with *Java*, a yellow Labrador, operational since 1992 and *Charley*, a beagle mix, operational since 1989. Both animals are qualified in search/cadaver work. All three dogs have previously successfully located human remains in actual searches.

Action Taken:

Traveled to Pensacola on January 28, 1995. Upon arrival, met with Special Agent Ray Dyal and Nancy Jones, and drove to inspect planned search areas. Actual search to commence on January 29, 1995.

1-29-93
0930–1230 hours Big Fish Point, off Big Fish Road, Santa Rosa County

Area searched included wooded area, parking areas, tidal flats between Big Fish Road and East Bay. Area popular area among local residents. Large amount of trash and building materials dumped in various locations. Handlers worked independently using Java and Marianne. During search, located deer and hog remains, however, no alerts noted from either dog consistent with location of human remains.

Reinforcement problem set up and run using decomposed human blood for scent source.

Temperature approximately 55 degrees, wind light and variable.

1350–1410 hours Backyard of residence at 2345 Red Dog Road, Santa Rosa County

Area of rear yard approximately 75' by 125'. Area worked with Marianne, no alerts noted. Yard completely fenced, so no adjacent areas done.

1-3-93
0900–1030 hours Residence at 4321 Mary Drive, Santa Rosa County

Residence is located west of the convenience store where victim was working the night she was last seen. At the time of her disappearance, lot was a building site, where the excavation had been done for the slab. Slab was poured after August 6,1991. Checked area at night and there is a streetlight next door that illuminates the lot at night. According to the owner of the house, light was in place in 1991.

Initial search done of lot and exterior of house with Marianne and Java. Slight interest noted along east wall near electrical feed. Used a probe to vent both sides of cement driveway and exterior of house foundation. Worked with dogs with negative results. Then dug three holes below footing and earth loosened with probe to release possible scent from under slab

Hole #1—Easterly side of house near electrical feed, 6' from southeasterly corner
Hole #2—Northerly side of house, 42" from northwesterly corner
Hole #3—Westerly side of house, 9' from the northwesterly corner.

One-half hour was allowed for scent to percolate and all three dogs were then worked again around the house. No alerts noted.

1100–1125 hours Deer Run Road, Santa Rosa County

Area between pond, river, and Deer Run Road searched by Nancy Jones using Charley and Java. Area wooded with some areas of heavy underbrush. No alerts noted. Covered from start of pond to end of cul-de-sac. Area measures approximately 60' by 500'.

CONCLUSION:
Based on the experience of the handlers and dogs used, it is the opinion of the writer that the dogs did not give any indication that any of the areas involved in this search contain any human remains. The search was conducted using recommended tactics and patterns, and several experienced dogs were worked in each area. Reinforcement training was done periodically with the animals to maintain a high level of motivation. No alerts were noted and no evidence of animal foraging was noted, except in those areas with recognizable animal remains.

HANDLER QUALIFICATIONS:

NANCY JONES	Member Northwest Florida Search & Rescue Association K-9 trainer since 1971; active as Search/Cadaver dog handler since 1989; has participated in over 25 searches; has made 9 recoveries. Graduate of Cadaver Dog Specialty Course, August 1992.
ANDREW REBMANN	Connecticut State Police Emergency Services Unit (retired) K-9 trainer since 1972, has participated in over 1000 searches during career; established Connecticut State Police Cadaver Dog program, dogs personally handled have made over 100 recoveries, currently operates K-9 Specialty Search School, Franklin, CT.
DATE OF REPORT:	February 16, 1993

EXAMPLE OF RECOVERY EXPANSION SEARCH REPORT

TO: Henry F. Ryan, M.D.
Chief Medical Examiner
Office of the Chief Medical Examiner

Sgt. Bob Smithson, CID III, Maine State Police

Sgt. Don Baxter, CID III, Maine State Police

Det. Barry Shepherd, CID III, Maine State Police

FR: Edward David, M.D., J.D., OCME

RE: Canine search: John Jones Homicide

I was contacted on 6-21-92 at 3:30 a.m. by PCO Levesque of the Orono Barracks at the request of Sgt. Bob Smithson. An informant, Jim Smith, had told Deputy Richard Wright of the County Sheriff's Office that he had witnessed and posibly been a party to a homicide committed in May of 1992. The victim was stated to be one John Jones of Our Town, Maine. The perpetrator was Bob Doe, aka Tiny. The Doe subject was stated to have shot Jones in the head with a .25 caliber semiautomatic pistol in the Lovely Lake area. He and Smith had then transported the body over Champion paper roads to a branch of the 48000 road where they had dug a shallow grave, placed the deceased in it, and then covered the grave and placed some brush over it. Based on this information, Det. Shepherd of the Maine State Police CID III took the Smith subject to Township 20. The Smith subject indicated the road and in fact a shallow excavated depression with some brush to the side was found. Some clothing was noted in this depression but there was no body.

I responded with Canines Wraith and Shadow to the scene in the company of Maine State Police Crime Lab personnel, Deputy Wright and Det. Shepherd at 7:25 a.m. 6/21/92. The temperature was in the mid 60s. There was a light, variable, primarily easterly wind with intermittent light rain falling. The location was at the end of a branch road of the 48000 road system (see map). There was a wood yarding area with a great deal of slash still remaining. There were several hills with spruce and mixed conifer growth. Bear sign was prominent as were several bear bait sites.

Initially, Canine Wraith was taken down a prominent animal trail towards a beaver impoundment. This was in a north-northwesterly direction. No alerts were made but Canine Wraith did become agitated approximately 150 yards along the trail. I, as handler however, directed the dog to continue on the trail. Finding nothing, Canine Wraith was returned to the vehicle and Canine Shadow was taken out and started approximately 50 yards to the east of the grave site in a north-northwesterly direction. Approximately 150 yards into the woods, Canine Shadow alerted on what proved to be a human pelvis, fibula, and two femurs. Canine Shadow continued her search pattern to the north and east, but made no further finds and was returned to the vehicle.

Canine Wraith was brought back to the grave site where Det. LaChance had found what he thought was some human hair somewhat west of the grave. Canine Wraith was put on this track and within five minutes (10:00 a.m.) alerted on the site of the matted and torn up moss perhaps 15 feet in diameter. This area contained the cranium, a piece of skin, blue jeans, shirt, and sneakers. Canine Wraith was returned to the vehicle and the Crime Lab collected physical evidence while this investigator collected the human remains.

Subsequently, Canine Wraith was again sent out this time from the area of principle find. A human humerus was located approximately 50 yards north of where the skull had been found. No other major finds were made. I cleared the scene at 12:30 p.m.

Map attached (not included here). Names have been changed.

APPENDIX C

RESUME EXAMPLES

HANDLER RESUME EXAMPLE A

ANDREW J. REBMANN
P.O. Box 5100
Kent, WA 98064-5100
Telephone (253) 630-0444

January 1991 to present:

Owner K-9 Specialty Search School, North Franklin, CT. Relocated to Redmond, WA in 1993. Provide instruction in cadaver search techniques for law enforcement and search and rescue personnel. Instruction includes both classroom and practical field work in conducting searches for human remains, both above ground and buried, evidence search, water search and man-trailing techniques.

Instructor of specialty seminars for search and rescue and law enforcement.

Recent seminars include:

- California Rescue Dog Association Basic Cadaver Search (October 1992)
- National K-9 Rescue School Search and Rescue Techniques (May 1991, September 1992)
- Federal Bureau of Investigation Detection and Recovery of Human Remains (September 1991, September 1992)
- Virginia Department of Emergency Services Basic Cadaver
- Search (August 1991)
- New England K-9 SAR Basic Cadaver Search (September 1991)
- National Police Bloodhound Association Training School (April 1991)
- Texas Homicide Symposium (May 1993)

- Missouri Search Dog Association Basic Cadaver Search (May 1993)
- National Association for Search and Rescue Conference (June 1993)
- Florida Search Dog Association (February 1994)

Recent Cadaver Search schools include four two-week sessions held in Connecticut between August 1992 and April 1993, for 24 students from 9 states. During August and September 1993, on-site two week cadaver search schools were inducted in Fairbanks, Alaska and Tualatin, Oregon

November 1970-January 1991 CONNECTICUT STATE POLICE
100 Washington Street
Hartford, CT
Trooper First Class

January 1977-January 1991 EMERGENCY SERVICES UNIT

Assigned a canine trainer, responsible for basic and in-service instruction for State Police and municipal Police handlers. Developed course materials and training techniques for 14-week basic patrol dog course.

Developed and instructed missing person search course for police, fire, and volunteer personnel. Active in training K-9s for patrol, drug detection, explosive detection, search and rescue, mantrailing and cadaver search.

In 1978, developed and implemented training program for cadaver search dogs, using chemical imprintation techniques. In 1986, developed and instructed three-week cadaver dog school for police officers. Handlers were trained from 15 out-of-state departments, along with 9 teams for Connecticut State Police. Personally handled cadaver dogs that have located over 100 bodies.

In 1973, assigned as bloodhound handler. Appointed Department bloodhound trainer in 1977. Responsible for acquisition, training and response to searches. Dogs trained and handled personally used in over 1000 searches, with an 80% success rate.

In 1986 developed and instructed a three-week bloodhound handlers course for law enforcement. Nineteen handlers from 12 outside departments completed the course. During State Police career, involved in search operations in 19 states, assisting local and state agencies and the Federal Bureau of Investigation

Qualified as an expert witness in the use of dogs for man-trailing in the Connecticut Courts.

Testimony has been upheld by the Connecticut Supreme Court in three cases. Search warrants have been issued on both bloodhounds and search/cadaver dogs. Have also testified in New York

State and the Commonwealth of Pennsylvania regarding residual scent.

As a member of the K-9 training staff contributed written chapters to CSP Training Manual. Developed department guidelines for conduct of missing person searches. Contributor to National Police Bloodhound Association training documents and newsletter. Contributor to National Search and Rescue Association conference proceedings regarding training techniques for cadaver dogs.

ADDITIONAL DUTIES

—Missing person search co-ordinator for department

—Trained radiological technician for industrial and transportation accidents

—Boat captain for marine patrol

—Provide public relations presentations for civic groups

—In conjunction with other members of the training staff, up-date instruction to state of the art, establish unit goals and annual budgets, maintain schedules

April 1971-January 1977 PATROL TROOPER

Troop E, Montville

Patrol assigned area to provide service and protection for the public. Investigate citizen complaints, reported crimes and motor vehicle accidents. Enforcement of motor vehicle and criminal laws. Writing of reports and testimony in court, when required.

November 1972

Assigned department patrol dog.

August 1973

Assigned department bloodhound

November 1970-April 1971

Connecticut State Police Academy, Groton, CT

PROFESSIONAL AFFILIATIONS

National Police Bloodhound Association

Member since 1974, officer from 1977 to 1984. Accredited instructor since 1979. Member of the training committee 1975 to present.

National Association For Search and Rescue

Member since 1978. Presented program on use of bloodhounds in SAR at National Conference, Baton Rouge, LA 1979. Presenter at 1993 National Conference, Tampa, FL.

National K-9 Rescue School

Instructor 1985, 1989, 1991, 1992

New England State Police Assistance Compact K-9 Trainers

Instructor for regional seminars since 1978

Northwest Disaster Search Dogs

Search and Rescue Dogs of the United States

Member, National Steering Committee since 1991

AWARDS

Connecticut State Police Meritorious Service Medal

Awarded 1972 and 1987

Connecticut State Police Medal for Outstanding Police Service

Awarded 1990

The "Cleopatra Big T" Award

Awarded by the National Police Bloodhound Association for the outstanding mantrailer in the field of law enforcement.

Awarded 1977

Sigma "Excellence in Training" Award

Presented by Sigma Chemical Company for accomplishments in the field of search and rescue.

Awarded 1993

Numerous citations from local and state police agencies for search assistance

References available on request

HANDLER RESUME
EXAMPLE B

MARCIA KOENIG
P.O. Box 625
Redmond, WA 98073
(206) 814-2291

Community College and high school teacher—biology, art
National Park Service—law enforcement ranger, 1986

Search and Rescue Experience

Founding member of Texas Search & Rescue Dogs - 1972-1980
Founding member American Rescue Dog Assn. - 1973
Training director - 3 years, Texas unit
Search & Rescue Dogs Assn. member (WA) - 1980-1984
German Shepherd Search Dogs of Washington - 1984-1991
Snohomish County Search and Rescue - 1990-1993
Pacific Rim Disaster Team - 1989-1990
Northwest Disaster Search Dogs - 1990-present
Puget Sound FEMA Task Force - 1992-present
Instructor to start Minneapolis, Minnesota dog unit - 1982
Instructor to start Victoria, British Columbia dog unit - 1987
Instructor to start Rochester, Minnesota dog unit - 1991
Guest instructor for Connecticut State Patrol K-9 Unit
SAR Canine School instructor - 1989, 1992
Canine Specialty Search Associates - 1993-present Instructor - four cadaver classes
National Assn. for Search and Rescue instructor - 1974-present
NASAR representative and speaker at International Rescue Symposium - Geilo, Norway 5/87
NASAR representative to 4th International Rescue Dog Symposium - Berlin, Germany 11/91
NASAR representative and speaker at 5th International Rescue Dog Symposium - Stockholm, Sweden 5/93
NASAR Chair, Search and Rescue Dog Committee 1992-present

AWARDS

Fellow - National Association for Search and Rescue

PUBLICATIONS

"Utilizing Dogs for Body Searches" 1984
"Wilderness Search Strategy for Dog Handlers" 1987
"Water Search on the Iowa River" 1988
"The ABCs of Dogs in Search & Rescue," Doran and Koenig 1989

"Handler Strategies for Water Search Scenes" 1990
Video "Developing the Reliable Jumper," Petersen and Koenig 1984
Video "Water Searching with Dogs" 1989
Videos in production, "Snow and Avalanche Searching with Dogs," "Cadaver Location with Dogs"

CANINE RESUME EXAMPLE

MARIANNE
Owner: Andrew J. Rebmann
P.O. Box 2083
Redmond, WA 98073

German Shepherd Female
Whelped: November 19, 1986

December 27, 1988
  Acquired by Connecticut State Police from Fidelco Guide Dog Foundation. Original name LEKA

January 1991
  Transferred to handler upon retirement

Health

Spayed	7-27-88	
Hips X-Rayed	6-9-87 Normal	
DHLPP	due 8-94	
Rabies	due 8-96	
Rhone Merieux, Inc.	IMRAB	
Serial No. 12111		
Rabies Tag No.	80398	
Lyme	4-94	
Heartworm test	4-94	negative
Bordetella	4-94	
Stool	3-93	negative

TRAINING

  Qualified as search/cadaver dog December 1989
  Used as backup for primary search/cadaver dog
    December 1989 to July 1992
  Primary search/cadaver dog July 1992 to present

EXPERIENCE

  Serial Murder Case, New Bedford, MA
    June 1990
  Person Search, New Britain CT
    September–October 1992
  Homicide Investigation, Mecklenburg County, VA
    (November 1992)
  Missing Hunter (Drowning), North Stonington, CT
    (December 1992)
  Speculative Homicide Search, Santa Rosa County, FL
    (January 1993)

Speculative Search, Tondre Homicide Case, Attleboro, MA
April 1993
Missing Person Search, Farmington, CT
April 1993
Speculative Search, Suicide Victim, New Britain, CT
May 1993
Speculative Homicide Search, Pensacola and Walton Counties, FL
June 1993
Evidence Search (Lost Bracelet), Wesley Chapel, FL
June 1993
Search for Drowning Victim, East Providence, RI
July 1993
Speculative Homicide Search, Exeter, RI
July 1993
Speculative Homicide Search, Walton County, FL
July 1993
Speculative Homicide Search (Land and Water), Clay County, MO
November 1993
Speculative Homicide Search, Walton County, FL
March 1994
Speculative Missing Person Search, The Dales, OR
April 1994
Speculative Homicide Search, Perry County, MO
May 1994

To date, SAR/cadaver dog has made one body location and has had a search warrant issued, based on her alerts.

TRAINING RECORD EXAMPLE

Andrew J. Rebmann
SEARCH/CADAVER DOG TRAINING RECORD

Date of training: May 18, 1994

Handler: A. Rebmann Dog: Marianne

Training location: Nike Base, Redmond

Terrain (type): Field (heavy vegetation)

Training aid used: Soil (RI 90-92); Pseudo™ Corpse

Date/time problem set: 5-18 1730

Time worked: 1845 Time delay: 1-1/4 hour

Time involved in search: 15 min.

Weather conditions: Fair Wind direction: westerly

Wind speed: 0-5 mph Temperature: 65° F

Other: Clear

Type problem: Live person search ( ) Above surface (x)
Hanging ( ) Water( ) Disaster( ) Buried( )
If buried: Depth: Type soil:

Description of problem:

1. PC1 hidden in tall grass off parking lot
2. Soil in tube hidden in scrub off large field. Both problems blind; set up by Marcy

Training aid located: Yes (x) No ( )

Comments on work of dog:

Good readable alert on both sources; performed refind with motivator. Problem #2 dog could not do sit alert because of heavy vegetation, so retrieved scent tube.

Date of report: 5/18/1994 Signature:

(Use reverse for additional comments or diagram of problem)

GLOSSARY

Accidental death — manner of death; when victim's death is caused by accident

Acclimate — to become accustomed to a different climate or environment

Active alert — dog's trained indication includes a more active behavior, such as digging, barking or scratching

Adipocere — waxy or soapy substance formed when the fats in animal bodies decompose, especially in moist environments; also called grave-wax

Air scenting — canine behavior with head held off the ground accompanied by nasal air exchange

Air scent search — search of a designated area by a canine trained to indicate the location of particular scents; includes searches for narcotics, land mines, agricultural products, missing persons, and dead persons

Alert — a trained behavioral indication given by the dog in response to locating the source of decomposition scent

Anchor point — a fixed, designated point used to orient the boundaries of a search

Anosmia — loss of capacity to smell odors

Artificial decomposition scent — chemicals produced commercially for scent training which reproduce compounds that occur during decomposition (putrescine and cadaverine)

Atrophy — loss of function due to age, disuse, or disease

Attitude change — alteration in the trained dog's demeanor when it senses the target odor, including an increased alertness and inquisitiveness

Autolysis — the destruction of cells after death due to lack of ability to metabolize oxygen needed by enzymes for cell activity

Axon — the part of an individual nerve cell along by which impulses travel from the nerve cell body

Behavior chain — the complete behavior including all of its steps, e.g., in wilderness work, the dog searches for the subject, finds the subject, returns to the handler and lets him know he has found the subject, leads the handler back to the subject, and is rewarded

Biological death — the cessation of all bodily functions

Blind area search — training routine where handler does not know where scent source is located

Boxing [the compass needle] — placing and keeping the magnetic needle within the outline of the orienting needle after you establish the direction of travel

Buried source — phase of training where dog is taught to indicate the location of scent coming from a buried source

Cadaver dog — canines specially trained to find human decomposition scent and alert their handlers to its location

Cadaverine — malodorous chemical compound produced during decomposition

Canid/canine — member of the family Canidae which includes dogs, coyotes, wolves, and foxes

Canine cadaver search — the investigation of a particular area deemed by forensic investigators to contain human remains according to a strategy designed for that particular context

Carnivore — animal that eats flesh; type of scavenger; canines, felines, raptors, and lobsters are examples

Casting — term used to refer to the initial search for a scent

Cause of death — the proximate pathological change responsible for death

Chain of custody — documentation of changes in the location and custody of evidence

Clicker — small, hand-held device that makes a clicking noise, used as a conditioned reinforcement to signal to the dog that it did the desired behavior and a reward is coming

Close grid search — pattern where dog works within 5-15 feet ahead of handler quartering the wind; handler can observe the dog

Command/cue — verbal command given by the trainer to commence a certain routine set of behaviors or task

Commissures — points of contact and communication linking information between right and left sides of the brain

Conditioned reinforcer — a signal or stimulus that has been paired with a positive reinforcement enough so that it has the same effect as the positive reinforcement; it means to the animal "you are doing the right thing;" for example words, whistle, clicker

Consent search — exception to the requirement for a search warrant; written or oral permission is required from a person with authority to give it

Corridor — arbitrary parallel paths to be traversed in searching an area, perpendicular to the search baseline and backline, and starting at the anchor point

Corridor search — see *Grid search*

Cortex — the outer layer of grey matter of the brain

Cross grid search — pattern in which dog works perpendicular to the previous search

Cue — signal provided by the trainer that a certain routine or set of behaviors is expected

Curtilage — that part of one's private property where he or she has an expectation of privacy to which society agrees; requires a warrant to search

Declination — the difference between true north as shown on a topographic map and magnetic north as indicated by the magnetic needle on a compass

Decomposition — chemical breakdown, separating compounds into their component parts; includes breakdown of proteins by putrefaction, of carbohydrates by fermentation, and of fats by rancidification

Dendrite — the branched part of a nerve cell that carries information toward the nerve cell body

Detailing — Conducting a close search, frequently on leash and under tight control of the handler

Disarticulation — the separation of joints due to the decomposition of soft tissue holding them together or to animal modification or transport

Distractors — challenges to the dog's ability to focus and/or to the accuracy of decomposition scent training, introduced to prepare the dog for distractions in a real search; usually non-human, animal remains

Down — a command to lie down; the behavior of lying down in response to a command

Downwind — a term used to describe the position of the searching dog team relative to the odor source, where the wind is blowing from the source toward the team

Drowning, dry — deaths from non-drowning causes where water did not fill the lungs

Drowning, wet — deaths from drowning where water fills the lungs

Exigent circumstances — exception to the requirement for a search warrant, when there is no time to get a warrant and failure to search will lead to destruction or concealment of evidence, injury to police or others, or escape of the suspect

False alert — dog gives trained indication, but no remains are found by humans

Fluency — ability of the dog to produce the trained behavior quickly and accurately.

Focused speculative search — type of canine cadaver search where remains are suspected to be in a fairly well-defined area

Forensic taphonomy — the study of postmortem processes affecting human remains for the purposes of interpreting forensic data.

Free search — pattern in which dog is allowed to roam throughout the area with no particular plan

GPS (Global Positioning Satellite) Receiver — hand-held device that indicates your geographic position by receiving radio signals from satellites in precise, fixed orbits around the earth

Grid search — particular search pattern that involves traversing parallel corridors, perpendicular to the wind if possible, so that the area is covered evenly; also termed corridor search or thorough searches

Hanging subject — training phase where dog is taught to locate a scent source above the ground

Hasty search — non-thorough search conducted to check out a large area quickly or in order to plan a thorough search

Hidden source — when target odor source is hidden from the dog's view but the dog is expected to find it; an early phase of training

Homicide — manner of death; when the death of one person is caused by the actions of another person, including manslaughter and murder

Horizontal scent cone — a scent cone formed with wind moving across a source and parallel to the ground, with the cone apex and greatest scent intensity nearest the source

Hot block — term used to describe the one cement block of several in a training set-up that contains the scent source

Imprinting — early phase of training that includes teaching scent recognition and scent commitment

Interdigital scent glands — scent glands between the toes in canines

Joint and several liability — when the group or any member of the group is considered liable for the actions of the group or any member of the group

Levels of certainty — judgement about search outcomes based on potential for scent cone distortion or weakening, thoroughness of coverage, dog efficacy, victim attributes, investigatory information base, and extraneous search factors; if remains are not found, the level of certainty cannot be 100 percent

Line-ups — a type of training or search routine set up to test a series of articles or vehicles for the presence of decomposition scent; also called scent line-ups

Livor mortis — settling of blood after death due to lack of circulation

Manner of death — a typology of deaths according to whether they are due to homicide, suicide, accident, or natural causes (see also cause of death)

Natural alert — natural behavior a particular dog exhibits when it comes in contact with the target odor, i.e., has entered the scent cone

Natural death — manner of death when due to natural disease or age

Natural decomposition scent — scent from decomposing human flesh, blood, adipocere, or other body fluid containing protein and/or fat

Negative area search — training routine where dog is taught to search an area despite the lack of a scent cone

Negative reinforcement — something the animal works to avoid

Negligence — an act or omission that causes harm despite duty to behave otherwise

Neuron — the primary unit of the nervous system, including the nerve cell body and all of its processes (an axon and one or more dendrites)

Non-focused speculative search — type of canine cadaver search where remains are suspected to be in a general area, without defined boundaries

Odorant — a substance possessing a perceptible odor

Off/on lead — term used to describe a search routine in which the canine is or is not leashed

Olfaction — the act of detecting scent, generally by respiration, transmitting impulses from the mucous membranes in the upper part of the nose via the olfactory nerve to the forebrain, where the information is translated into perceived odors

Olfactory bulb — the part of the brain that aggregates scent stimuli and transmits them to the olfactory cortex; also called olfactory tubercle

Olfactory nerve — the first cranial nerve pair, connecting receptor cells from each side of the nose to the brain

Olfactory peduncle — a stemlike or constricted part of the brain that bears the olfactory lobe

Omnivores — animals that eat both flesh and plants routinely; type of scavenger; bears, rodents, and corvids (crows and ravens) are examples

Open grid search — pattern where dog works 25–50 feet ahead of handler quartering the wind

Operant conditioning — shaping a particular behavior by pairing a particular stimulus and response with a reinforcement

Outside corridor line — an arbitrary line set up to bound the search area, connected to the anchor point, and perpendicular to the search baseline; this line is the edge of the first corridor to be searched

Passive alert — dog's trained indication is relatively inactive, such as a sit or down; may be preferred to an active alert to protect a crime scene from disturbance

Plain view — an exception to the requirement for a search warrant, when there is evidence of a crime in plain view by a person who sees it lawfully

Positive reinforcement — a stimulus perceived as positive to the animal being trained; something the animal will work to get, such as food, petting, play

Prey drive — the behavioral tendency of a canine to pursue prey (or prey-substitutes such as balls) compared with other, potentially competing, drives

Primary alert — trained indication the dog gives when it finds the target scent source

Primary olfactory pathway — the anatomical route by which odor stimuli are transmitted to the brain via the nerves

Primary scent pool — distribution of scent molecules around a source prior to significant diffusion by wind or water

Primary reinforcer — something that works on the animal without being taught (positive: food, play, petting, instinctive behavior; negative: pain, distasteful substance or odor)

Probable cause — justification required to obtain a search warrant

Probe — a device used to penetrate the ground to a depth of one or more feet in order to release odor for perception by the dog in the search for buried remains

Putrefaction and fermentation — breakdown of tissues, particularly proteins, due to enzyme action

Putrescine — malodorous chemical compound produced during decomposition

Qualify the witness — process of establishing the qualifications of the witness to give a particular type of testimony; includes expert testimony of the handler and the "expertise" of the trained K-9

Quartering the wind — search pattern which involves traversing a path perpendicular to wind direction

Reading the dog — observing the dog's behavior closely to detect an attitude change when it encounters the target odor

Recovery expansion search — type of canine cadaver search where some remains have already been discovered and additional remains are sought from that area

Refind — trained behavior when canine finds the scent, comes to the trainer, gives some indication it has found the target scent, and is cued to take the handler back to that target

Reinforcement — anything that affects behavior due to association with that behavior; in canine training, reinforcement provides information to the dog about the correctness of what it is doing

Resumé — a formal summary and documentation of training and experience of handler and of individual dogs; sometimes termed a c.v., vita, or curriculum vitae

Rigor mortis — the stiffening of the body hours after death, lasting several days

Scavenger — animal that feeds on dead animals; includes carnivores and omnivores in both terrestrial and aqueous environments

Scent cage — container for scent to be used in training for water searches, such as a cricket cage used commonly by fishermen; see *Training containers*

Scent commitment — phase of training that requires the dog to strengthen its recognition of the target odor

Scent cone — the patterned distribution of scent molecules that have diffused from a source, generally becoming less concentrated and more dispersed the further from the source they diffuse

Scent cone distortion — alteration in scent cone shape or concentration due to variation in wind direction or air flow barriers

Scent line-ups — see *Line-ups*

Scent pump — see *Training containers*

Scent recognition — early phase of scent training which requires the dog to recognize the target scent as different from others

Scent tube — see *Training containers*

Scent void — absence of scent molecules within a theoretical scent cone distribution pattern

Schutzen — a type of competitive training for dogs emphasizing both obedience and endurance

Search and rescue — search, often by dog/handler teams, for individuals who are missing and may need to be rescued; frequently includes the possibility the missing individuals are dead

Search and seizure — form of investigation covered by the Fourth Amendment, requiring the area searched to be free from the reasonable expectation of privacy unless there is a search warrant

Search baseline — an arbitrary boundary of an area to be searched, perpendicular to the route of travel and parallel to the backline

Search report — a formal report detailing a canine search, including background, conduct of the search, and results

Secondary alert — see *Natural alert*

Secondary scent cone — scent cone formed when wind-borne scent molecules change direction, pool, and diffuse in a different direction

Secondary scent pool — pool of scent formed remote from the source when wind-borne scent molecules pool at air flow barriers

Shaping behavior — act of training an animal to produce a certain behavior by pairing it with a positive or negative reinforcement

Shaping behavior — the progressive changing of behavior (see also operant conditioning)

Skeletonization — the exposure of the bones of the skeleton due to the loss of soft tissue during decomposition

Spiral search — pattern in which dog is worked in a circle pattern from a specific point

Spot search — handler chooses areas with higher likelihood in an otherwise unfocused search; might include areas accessible by vehicles, footpaths, or refuse areas

Strict liability — criminal sanction imposed without requiring a showing of intent, e.g., being liable for a dog's misbehavior

Subpoena — a court document commanding a person to appear at a certain time and place to give testimony on a certain matter, or to produce written material or other items

Suicide — manner of death; when the death of a person is caused by his or her own actions

Synapse — point of contact and communication between neurons

Taphonomic agents — biological, chemical, and geological processes that influence postmortem change

Target odor — a specific type of odor that the dog is being trained to locate and indicate

Thalamus — part of the brain that is usually the main relay center for sensory impulses to the cerebral cortex, but which is bypassed in canine olfaction

Thermal uplift — rising heat due to differential temperature layers, generally in the absence of wind

Thorough search — see *Grid search*

Topographic map — a map that includes the geophysical variation of the land

Tort — wrongful act or omission

Tracking/trailing — canine behavior in which dog continues to walk with nose held close to the ground and sniffing or with obvious nasal air exchange

Trained indication — canine behavior that reliably indicates to the trainer that the scent source has been located; alert

Training containers — containers used for hiding and dispensing a scent source; includes scent tube, scent cage, and scent pump; also recycled glass, plastic, or metal containers with perforated covers

Training log — chronological documentation of the training activities undertaken by a K-9 team

Up-wind — a term used to describe the position of the searching dog team relative to the odor source, where the wind is blowing from the team toward the source

Vehicle search — type of search in which dog must check all areas of a vehicle

Vertical scent cone — scent cone formed in the absence of wind, with rising heat (thermal uplift), which carries molecules upward where they become more diffused

INDEX

C

D

H

I

J

K

L

M

N

O

P

T

Z